PSYCHOANALYTIC TECHNIQUE
AND PSYCHIC CONFLICT

CHARLES BRENNER, M.D.

INTERNATIONAL UNIVERSITIES PRESS, INC.
Madison, Connecticut

Fifth Printing, 1994

Library of Congress Cataloging in Publication Data

Brenner, Charles, 1913-
    Psychoanalytic technique and psychic conflict.

    Bibliography: p.
    Includes index.
    1. Psychoanalysis.   2. Conflict (Psychology)
I. Title.
RC506.B69   616.8'917   76-15047
ISBN 0-8236-5054-5

CONTENTS

FOREWORD

Dr. Charles Brenner needs no introduction to psycho-analytic readers. He is widely known, both in this country and abroad, as a clinician, theorist, and teacher. His writings are noted for clarity of thought, lucidity of exposition, and the consistent effort to support theory by clinical observation. This book is a further example of these qualities.

It is not a book of rules and precepts. Dr. Brenner approaches the problem of psychoanalytic technique by presenting the basic principles of the psychoanalytic method, the psychoanalytic attitude, and the relation of theory to practice. He speaks of "the awareness of the nature of the analytic task as a whole—the task of under-standing as fully as possible the nature and origins of each patient's conflicts." The statement and the theme—the ubiquitous and central importance of psychic conflict—are deceptively simple. However obvious they may seem at first glance, the reader of this book will find them developed here in a way that is profoundly significant and that deserves the most careful attention.

Dr. Brenner defends the scientific value of psycho-analytic technique in its clinical application, and throughout the book his theoretical formulations are richly supported by clinical illustrations.

In earlier publications Dr. Brenner has proposed new approaches to basic psychoanalytic concepts which he here applies to psychoanalytic technique. These include the theory of affects, transference and the therapeutic alliance, dreams, and, above all, the nature of conflict. He has demonstrated that many aspects of these important topics, hitherto taken for granted by psychoanalysts, require restatement, reappraisal, and the exercise of critical judgment that is based on a fresh view of the relevant clinical data. In this book he has collected much that has heretofore been scattered among various papers, has restated some of it with suitable emphasis on what he considers most directly applicable to technical problems, and has amplified and expanded the rest in a way that will engage the interest of every practicing analyst.

It is to an audience of "practicing analysts, present and future" that Dr. Brenner addresses himself. His book will enlighten the student; it will refresh and stimulate the graduate and even the senior analyst. For the nonanalyst it will be a clear indication of what psychoanalysis is all about.

David Beres, M.D.

New York
April, 1976

INTRODUCTION

This book is intended for practicing analysts, present and future. It is directed to every professional student of psychoanalytic technique. But it is not an attempt to teach the practice of psychoanalysis in a thorough or systematic way. For reasons that appear below, I doubt that any book is adequate to such a purpose.

The selection of the topics that are discussed and the content of the discussion are the result of a personal decision in every case. In general, I have followed two aims, first, to stick to the subject of technique, and, second, to omit what I believe to be common knowledge. Thus the book is a very personal contribution to the subject. It does not contain a detailed presentation of the many contributions made by other analytic authors, beginning with Freud, nor will the reader find here a systematic or critical review of those contributions.

The general plan of the book and the sequence in which the material is presented derive from the importance of the relationship between psychoanalytic technique and psychoanalytic theory. The fact bears frequent repetition that psychoanalytic technique, like any other scientifically based procedure, is not simply a collection of traditional precepts or rules of thumb (Brenner, 1969b). It is, on the contrary, an application of psychoanalytic theories of mental functioning and development to the practical problem of attempting in a special way to alter that functioning in an individual case. In addition, it is in fact both a principal source of the data on which those theories are based, and a constant test as well as a potential corrective of them.

It's obvious that there is nothing original or unusual about emphasizing the close relationship that exists between psychoanalytic technique and psychoanalytic theory. This has been done often and well in the past. The fact that the relationship is such a close one, however, has certain consequences for any theoretically based discussion of psychoanalytic technique. Whoever writes such a discussion is obligated to indicate to his readers, at least in a general way, what his own theoretical orientation is.

In my case this is easy to do. Any interested reader can find it expressed in considerable detail in earlier writings (Arlow and Brenner, 1964; Brenner, 1966, 1968a, 1968b, 1969a, 1969b, 1970, 1971, 1973a, 1974b, 1975a). The following summary may be useful nevertheless. It will be apparent that it follows the structural theory of Freud (1920, 1923a, 1926, 1933), and that it emphasizes as being of central importance in clinical work the part of the structural theory that has to do with psychic conflict.

Freud assumed that the mind is impelled to activity

by the energy of instinctual drives, whence the name
"drive." These drives are of two sorts, libidinal and aggressive. He also assumed that the mind itself is an apparatus—the mental or psychic apparatus—for the dis-
charge, control, and regulation of the instinctual energy
that drives it to activity. In its activity the psychic apparatus follows what Freud called the pleasure-unpleasure
principle, i.e., it seeks to achieve pleasure, particularly
the pleasure of instinctual gratification, and to avoid
unpleasure, particularly the unpleasure of instinctual
frustration and of anxiety.

Following Freud, the psychic apparatus is divided
into three parts, three structures, or, if you will, three
agencies called, respectively, the id, the ego, and the
superego. The id includes the instinctual, driving part of
the mind; the ego, the part that has to do with the outer
world; and the superego, the moral part. The justifica-
tion for making this division and its usefulness as a psychological theory derive from what one can observe in
situations of psychic conflict. Such conflicts are, broadly
speaking, of three kinds. In the first, one or more instinctual drive derivatives are opposed by the more mature,
the more organized, and the more coherent part of the
mind. In such cases the superego, if it is already formed
and functioning, is on the side of the more organized and
coherent part of the mind. In the second kind of conflict
the organized part of the personality is in conflict with an
unconscious need for self-punishment. In the third, the
self-punitive trend has become allied with a masochistic
wish and the two together are in conflict with the more
mature and organized part of the personality. In the
language of the structural theory, then, conflicts are

between id and ego (+ superego), between superego and ego, and between id + superego and ego. Thus the concepts and terminology of the structural theory reflect the importance attached to the role of conflict in mental life. There will be numerous occasions in the body of the book itself for much more to be said on the subject of conflict. For the moment this brief statement will do.

There are other attributes of the mental apparatus that are important enough to be mentioned here. One is the principle of psychic determinism. According to that principle, what is happening at any given moment in the mind is the result of what happened before, i.e., in the psychic as in the physical world, the determinism of cause and effect holds true. Another is the concept of the dynamic significance of unconscious psychic activity. In other words, what is unconscious may be as important a psychic determinant as what is conscious, or even much more important. Still another is the genetic principle, i.e., the assumption that the characteristics of the psychic apparatus in adult life are genetically related to the instinctual conflicts of childhood and to the events associated with them. Finally, there is the principle of multiple function (Waelder, 1930), according to which the consequences of psychic activity in general—thoughts, fantasies, actions, neurotic symptoms, etc.—are a compromise among id, ego, and superego. They are to some degree instinctually gratifying, to some degree defensive, to some degree influenced by moral considerations, and to some degree influenced by external reality. This last attribute of the psychic apparatus, i.e., compromise formation, will also be referred to frequently in what follows.

So much by way of a theoretical summary. It will serve, at least in a preliminary way, to orient readers for whom such an orientation is necessary. There is, in addition, one other point I wish to make as a prelude to the book itself, since I believe it to be quite as fundamentally important as is the theoretical orientation that underlies the book. Though this second point is anything but a theoretical one, it also requires a bit of explanation.

Psychoanalysis as a therapeutic procedure is a form of psychotherapy (Freud, 1904). The way to learn how to do it — psychoanalytic technique — is to psychoanalyze patients, at first with the help of frequent and regular consultations with a skilled and experienced colleague. In addition to this type of instruction, usually called supervision, case presentations to professional peers are educationally valuable, as are seminars at which the progress of treatment of a case in analysis is discussed at regular intervals both by peers and by more experienced colleagues. Even informal or anecdotal case discussions may be helpful at times, so that one may say that any clinical analytic discussion is likely to contribute something toward improving one's technique, though unquestionably the greatest contributions will come from presenting and discussing one's own cases.

Why should it be that one always learns so much more from a case of one's own than from the report of a case of someone else? Is it because so few analysts have the ability to present a case so that it really "comes alive"? I think not. Reading even the classic case reports of Freud cannot compare with regular consultations about a case of one's own as a way of learning technique. Even from Freud's case histories an eager student will catch no more than glimpses of "how Freud did it." From reports by less gifted writers one learns even less, but if one stops to ask why, the answer is not one that reflects discredit either on

Freud or on those who have followed his lead. With each of one's own supervised cases one spends every year between 200 and 250 sessions, each nearly an hour long, plus 40 to 50 sessions in consultation. In addition, one spends an indeterminate but considerable amount of extra time in thinking about the case, in making notes to be used in consultation, and in discussing the case informally with one's colleagues. The result of all this is a familiarity with the details of the case — both the history before analysis began and the progress of analysis itself — that is incomparably more thorough, more nearly complete, than is ever possible with a colleague's case. The closest one could ever come would be by participating in a continuous case seminar and in fact most analysts agree that, next to their own cases, they learned most about technique from such seminars. Even to think of spending many hundreds or a few thousands of hours studying a case report is enough to convince one that no such report can hope to compare in educational value with a case of one's own. And if one adds to these considerations, as one must, the fact that a case of one's own is always more interesting than anyone else's case for unconscious reasons, as well as for conscious ones, its advantages as an educational experience become even clearer. There is simply nothing quite like the experience of understanding something about a case of one's own that one didn't understand before — of forming a conjecture oneself and of having that conjecture confirmed by a patient's subsequent associations, behavior, or both.

Still, the printed word has its value for a student of analytic technique, even though it can never substitute for personal practical experience. Once one has acquired a moderate degree of familiarity with the practice of analysis and some skill in analytic technique one can learn a good deal both from vignettes or case reports and from general discussions of clinical problems. An author can hope, therefore, that a book on technique will serve a useful purpose, even though he recognizes that it can never do more than supplement a reader's personal experience as a clinician. This book is intended to furnish such a supplement. No book can do more.

1

PSYCHIC CONFLICT AND THE TASK OF THE ANALYST

I shall start with some aspects of psychic conflict. Familiar as this subject is to every student of psychoanalysis, some of the consequences of our knowledge of its origins, its nature, and its effects in mental functioning are so important to psychoanalytic technique that they are worth reviewing, even though much of the review will cover ground that is already well known to every reader.

The following summary from an earlier paper will serve to open our discussion.

> Since the publication of *Inhibitions, Symptoms and Anxiety* (Freud, 1926) anxiety has been the affect most closely associated with psychic conflict. The currently accepted connection between the two can be summarized as follows. Whenever a derivative of a drive or a self-punitive or self-destructive trend is perceived as dangerous, anxiety develops. In order

to eliminate or minimize this anxiety, attempts are made to ward off the dangerous derivative, i.e., to defend against it. The result is characteristically a compromise between derivative and defense, either with no anxiety or with less than would have developed without the defense. Thus the components of conflict are (1) wishful striving, (2) anticipated danger, (3) defense and (4) compromise among these. The function of defense is to avoid anxiety in accordance with the pleasure principle. Since current psychoanalytic theory—the structural theory—subsumes drive derivatives under the id, self-punitive trends under the superego and defenses under the ego, one may say that there are two major classes of conflict, those between ego and id and those between ego and superego. In both, anxiety is understood to occupy a key position. It is the trigger that sets an individual at odds with dangerous id or superego derivatives and that is responsible for the initiation of the defenses that oppose them [Brenner, 1975a, p. 5].

When I wrote the passage just quoted I believed I was merely formulating the currently accepted psychoanalytic view on the subject of conflict. Discussions with colleagues, however, revealed that some analysts customarily define conflict somewhat differently or, at any rate, more narrowly. One opinion expressed was that, of the complicated interaction of wishes, fears, and defenses that determines so much of human thought and behavior, only the reaction of anxiety or guilt should be called conflict. Another, that conflict means the presence of defenses against dangerous wishes and that neither anxiety nor guilt is to be included in the definition. It may be remarked in passing that the first of these definitions is essentially a subjective one, while the second is based rather on objective criteria. "I am in conflict about that" does often mean "That frightens me," or "That makes me feel guilty." Unconscious wishes and defenses against them, on the other hand, must be inferred by an observer, e.g., an analyst. They are not perceived by the subject (patient) himself.

It will also be noted that the definition of conflict with which I began this chapter is broader than either of the two just given. It includes both of them, in fact, and more besides. My reasons for preferring it to any narrower, less inclusive definition are these. When defenses are used to counter a dangerous instinctual wish or superego demand in order to avoid anxiety, it is the resulting compromise formation that appears in an individual's mental life and behavior as an observable phenomenon. It is the compromise that one hears and perceives as one listens to and observes a patient. Wish, anxiety, guilt, and defense all enter into the final result—the compromise—in every case, though the relative importance of each varies from one instance to another. The compromise is invariably the result of the interaction of them all.

It is because what one observes is an amalgam of the interacting elements just mentioned that it is advantageous to include all of them under the heading of psychic conflict. Wish, anxiety, guilt, and defense are the elements of every conflict. It is they that unite to form the final result. In other words, what is called a compromise formation is, to the best of our present knowledge, a consequence of wish, anxiety, guilt, and defense in varying proportions. To exclude any of them from a definition of conflict does violence to this fact. It may be added, for the sake of completeness, that a compromise formation is often influenced by current environmental circumstances as well.

One further word of explanation is necessary before we turn from matters of definition to those more practical considerations that are our principal concern. In the discussion of conflict in this chapter I shall limit to anxiety and guilt the affects that are responsible for initiating conflict. I have recently (1975a) offered evidence to support an expansion of this view, i.e., of the view that has been generally agreed on till now. The modification I have proposed and its application to psychoanalytic technique will be discussed in Chapter 4. To introduce it here would unnecessarily complicate the exposition of the ideas that are of primary importance in this chapter. With this reservation, then, we can turn now to some clinical applications of the definition of psychic conflict.

Let us assume an example in which the compromise formation is a neurotic symptom. In accordance with the ideas just summarized we must conclude that whatever conscious anxiety or guilt is associated with the symptom really derives from the wish that gave rise to the conflict and that it is conscious because the defense(s) against the wish were only partially successful. Thus, for example, if a patient is anxious when he is in a stalled bus, we attribute his anxiety to the unconscious wishes that are active in his mind at the time and not to whatever rationalization he may offer, e.g., that he's afraid because he can't get out or because there may not be enough air. If, to continue the example, the patient's frightening wish derives from a childhood fantasy of being inside his mother's body, we say that displacing the wish from mother to bus was not a good enough defense to prevent the emergence of at least some anxiety.

In other cases, however, some analysts tend to be less consistent in this regard. If a self-destructive patient is afraid that he will kill himself or if another patient has feelings of unreality accompanied by anxiety, one may find that an analyst tends to follow the patient's rationalizations rather than being guided by his own knowledge of the role of anxiety and guilt in mental life. Instead of directing his attention to the task of discovering the elements of the psychic conflict responsible for both the patient's symptom and for his anxiety and guilt, he may take the latter at face value, so to speak, and follow the patient's lead in attributing anxiety (or guilt) to the symptom rather than to the conflict that underlies it.

One can only speculate about why this should be so. The most important reasons are probably not readily accessible and not easily admitted, e.g., an unconscious reluctance to deal with a patient's conflicts because of the anxiety they threaten to arouse in oneself. Other reasons, more easily accessible, doubtless include a tendency to identify with the patient: "Who wouldn't be frightened by wanting to kill himself? Who wouldn't be scared if he felt everything was unreal?" A more sophisticated reason derives from the idea that "dissolution of ego organization" is something everyone fears and that "going crazy" or "feeling unreal" are frightening because they imply or portend such a dissolution.

Closely related to this last reason is the idea that psychotic symptoms are different from neurotic ones, that they are not compromise formations at all, but true "endopsychic perceptions" (Freud, 1911, p. 79), and are therefore to be taken at face value rather than analyzed as a neurotic symptom must be. Since suicidal impulses, for example, are common among psychotic patients, the belief that at least some psychotic symptoms are endopsychic perceptions tends to lead one to the notion that patients with suicidal thoughts that are accompanied by conscious anxiety are correct in attributing their anxiety to their conscious thoughts about killing themselves. If suicidal thoughts really were reliable endopsychic perceptions, if they really were simply a patient's accurate perceptions of what was happening in his mind, one could indeed explain them with some degree of plausibility as being due to the patient's awareness that his aggression had become directed against himself as an impulse to kill himself. One could at the same time attribute whatever anxiety accompanied a patient's suicidal thoughts to the fact that he unconsciously perceived that his aggression had turned, or had been turned, against himself. To reason in this way, however, is to lose sight of the fact that the psychic situation is, in fact, quite different. From our knowledge of psychic conflict we have every reason to expect that in the case of suicidal thoughts, as in the case of all other symptoms with which we are familiar, both the thoughts and the accompanying anxiety are derivatives of conflict, and clinical experience bears out our expectation. The same holds true for patients with feelings of unreality. Such feelings are not due to the correct perception by a patient that his ego organization is threatened with dissolution by the regressive process of his illness. They are compromise formations that, like other symptoms, derive from psychic conflict and so does whatever conscious anxiety may appear as an accompaniment to them.[1]

To repeat, we see that when a patient has thoughts or symptoms that his analyst associates with or attributes to severe mental illness there is a tendency to inconsistency

---

[1] For a fuller description see Arlow and Brenner (1964, Chapter 10).

on the part of some analysts in applying their knowledge of psychic conflict to the task of understanding the origin of the anxiety that the patient consciously experiences. Instead of attributing such a patient's anxiety to wishes that give rise to conflict in his mind because of the anxiety they arouse, as one would invariably do in the case of other, so-called neurotic symptoms, there is a tendency to attribute the patient's anxiety to the aspect of his conflict he is aware of as a symptom, i.e., to a part of the compromise formation that is conscious.

A similar inconsistent tendency is noticeable in connection with phenomena at the other end of the scale of severity of psychopathology, i.e., in connection with phenomena that fall within the realm of normality. For example, if a patient feels guilty about failing to live up to his own and his parents' expectations of him, one is likely to say, "Of course, that's reality," and to neglect the truly important sources of his conscious affect, namely, the guilt-provoking wishes connected with his failure, wishes that may even have been responsible for his having failed in the first place. Similarly, if a patient is made anxious by something that was quite beyond his control and unquestionably "real," like a physical illness, an accident, or a financial reversal, an analyst may tend to attribute his patient's anxiety, as the patient himself does, to the "reality" of the situation rather than to the more important psychic reality, i.e., to the consonance between the external situation and the patient's own, often unconscious, anxiety-laden wishes.

Here again the reasons for an analyst's failure to apply his knowledge of psychic conflict in a consistent way are often individual and inaccessible except through analysis of the analyst himself. In addition, identification may also play a part: "It's only natural to feel that way. I would if it were I." Perhaps a part is sometimes played as well by the idea that there are two *kinds* of anxiety, the one neurotic and the other "realistic," an idea, incidentally, to which Freud himself subscribed before 1926. Whatever its reasons, the tendency to inconsistency is there with respect to "normal" mental reactions just as it is with respect to "psychotic" ones.

Why such an extensive discussion of inconsistencies in the application of one's understanding of psychic conflict to various symptomatic and normal phenomena? What does it have to do with the subject in which we are interested, psychoanalytic technique? Suppose an analyst is occasionally inconsistent in ways like these. What effect will it have on his ability to conduct an analysis?

The answer is, "Often none at all, but sometimes a great deal." For example, when a patient reports ideas of dying or of killing himself that, he says, frighten him, it is important to understand that both the suicidal ideas and the anxiety are consequences of a conflict of which the patient himself is wholly or partly unaware and which, even if he is partly aware of it, he does not connect to its consequences. Suicidal thoughts are fantasies which are more or less fully elaborated and which, like any fantasies or, for that matter, like any conscious thoughts, are compromise formations. When one understands this it is obvious how one should proceed technically when a patient in analysis reports such thoughts. One should induce the patient to report them as fully as possible and then to associate to them as freely as he can.

An abbreviated example may be helpful. The patient was a man with a long history of recurrent depression and self-defeating behavior. He made a suicidal attempt shortly before starting treatment, an attempt that he dismissed as play acting, though in fact it might well have succeeded if a friend had not intervened. As would be expected, suicidal thoughts were frequent during his analysis. He characteristically either minimized their importance or failed to report them altogether. Thus he might say, "Oh, yes. I've been thinking of suicide off and on for the past couple of weeks, but at the time it was happening I really hardly noticed it." There were doubtless several motives for his defending against awareness of his suicidal thoughts as he did, but one motive became abundantly clear in the course of the analysis: to admit how sick he was meant realizing how much he needed analysis and that meant being intolerably dependent on his analyst who, he feared, might leave him as had his father, who died when he was three, his grandfather, who left the household when he was six, and a teacher who died suddenly when the patient was 25 and on whom the patient had felt quite dependent for advice and encouragement for five or six years before that. Even worse than the fear that his analyst might leave him were two other, closely related fears. The first was that in his rage he himself might leave first or might kill his analyst. The second, the dread of coming to his analyst in tears, begging for love like a supplicant, like a woman.

Much time was spent during the early months of this patient's analysis in analyzing his defenses against his frightening wish for his analyst to love him. As a result he was eventually able to be conscious much more than he had been at first of many of its nonsensual aspects. He could express feelings of admiration, of a desire to be admired in turn, of pleasure in discussing topics of mutual interest, and of gratitude for help that he felt he had gained from analysis. It then became apparent that he was unhappy, worried, and had suicidal thoughts during each weekend separation from his analyst. At times he feared that none of the jobs he was negotiating for would materialize, at times he was sure that they wouldn't. Despite his comfortable financial circumstances he feared poverty and even thought of the possibility of starvation. He repeatedly thought of economizing by leaving analysis or at least reducing the number of analytic sessions each week. At times he thought, "It's too much. I'm tired," by which he understood himself to mean that he was tired of living. Once or twice he said to a friend, "Maybe I should cash in my chips," pretending that he was only joking but well aware himself that he was very serious. All of this was told during his session on Monday and to some extent on Tuesday, but by the end of the week he was quite cheerful, confident about his job prospects and in general optimistic. After this sequence had been observed for three weeks it was called to his attention on a Friday along with a suggestion that it might be that he missed me during the weekend. On the following Monday he returned with the information that the events of the weekend did not support my observation of the Friday before. He had been neither depressed, he said, nor aware of suicidal thoughts. It was clear that he thought me wrong in my guess. He had a dream to report, however. In his dream he was in a ranch-style house. His girlfriend was with him and he behaved in her presence in a way that he should have known would make her jealous. Sure enough, she disappeared and he wandered through the building vainly seeking her. Finally, however, he was able to find her. He was surprised and relieved to discover that she was not angry, but it was clear that she was leaving him forever. His associations had principally to do with his guilt at having arranged a meeting for later in the week with another woman. He felt terrible about deceiving his girl-friend—it was a stupid thing to do, why did he persist in such behavior—maybe he was planning to desert her in the end, even though she was by far the best girl he had ever known and he should really settle down and marry her. When he was questioned about the building, he was puzzled at first, but finally realized that the most striking thing about it was how horizontal it was. It was just the opposite of a high-rise apartment like the one in which he lived at the time his father died and which he had recently driven past. As he left his analytic hour he remarked that it must surely have been the shortest 50 minutes that ever were. On the following day he reported that he had again failed to live up to my prediction. Instead of feeling better, he had suddenly become very depressed the afternoon before: "Everything turned black suddenly. Not physically of course." After he had spoken for some time of his discouragement about his career, about how poor he felt, about his thoughts about starving and about stopping analysis in order to save money, I reminded him of the dream he had told me about the day before and suggested that it expressed the thought that he was *not* going to run the risk of having me leave him as his father had done, that *he* was going to do the leaving this time and his girl-friend would be the one who felt lonely, unhappy, and furious, not he. He responded by talking again of his compulsion to be unfaithful and of his guilt at acting so. He also revealed that fantasies of pleading with older men friends—not with me—for help and advice had much occupied his thoughts during this most recent period of depression. I reminded him how like a girl it made him feel to think of pleading for me to love and help him, and from what he said it was apparent that the suicidal thoughts he had had since the previous afternoon were unconsciously intended to win him sympathy and love. At the same time his sarcastic and jokingly argumentative responses to much of what I said—responses that were quite different from his usual way of speaking—revealed how angry he was and what efforts he made to conceal it.

One can conclude from these data that the patient's suicidal thoughts derived in part from each of the following sources. (1) A wish (conscious throughout his childhood) that his father were alive and loved him. (2) Identification with his dead father, of whom he had been told both that he was an avid poker player ("I should cash in my chips") and that he had complained of feeling tired during the months before his death. (3) A wish to be a girl so that his analyst (= father; grandfather) would love him. (4) A wish to kill or abandon his analyst (= father; grandfather) for leaving him. (5) Substitution of girlfriend for analyst (= mother for father) so that *he* would be the man and take revenge on women by leaving them. This, incidentally, is one determinant of his identification with his father. (6) A need to punish himself for his murderous and incestuous wishes and actions. (7) A need to defend himself against, i.e., to try to ward off, his murderous, incestuous, and self-punitive wishes and needs. Prominent among his defenses were repression, displacement, identification in order to turn passive into active and to undo or prevent castration, turning of aggression against himself, denial, and isolation of affect.

This brief report is intended to illustrate two points about the patient. First, that his suicidal thoughts, as well as the accompanying thoughts of failure and destitution, his dream, and his sexual behavior were indeed a set of multiply determined compromise formations that resulted from the same psychic conflict or from a group of closely related conflicts, and, second, that the psychic forces responsible for the entire set of related thoughts and symptoms in question could be inferred from the usual analytic data and from them alone. One could understand the patient's symptoms and their origin only by learning of the conflicts that underlay them, and one could infer the underlying conflicts only if the patient told his symptoms and associated to them, to his dream, and to his sexual behavior.

One can understand from this report, then, how important it is to be consistent in applying one's knowledge of psychic conflict and its consequences. It is only in cases in which suicidal, or, more generally, self-destructive and self-defeating tendencies are of relatively little importance that it does not much matter if one's attitude toward them is consistent with one's knowledge of psychic conflict or not. When such tendencies are of major importance, as in the case just given, it is essential to be consistent in applying one's knowledge of the nature and role of psychic conflict to the task of analyzing those tendencies. Failure to do so will inevitably lead to major difficulties in the analysis. Either the analysis will fail, possibly because the patient kills himself or because he interrupts his analysis on some pretext, or it will flounder to a less than satisfactory conclusion. It is not likely to be very useful to tell a patient like the one just described simply that he is "turning his aggression against himself," or that he is "depressed because he is guilty" and that his fears of poverty and starvation result from his "oral greed," or even that his suicidal thoughts represent a wish to be united with his dead father. Such stock explanations can play no more than a minor role at best in one's interpretive efforts. However true they may be they are clearly inadequate to the analytic task of helping the patient to understand the nature and origin of *his* pathogenic conflicts—wishes, fears, self-punishment, and defenses—well enough so that his symptoms will substantially ameliorate or even, perhaps, disappear. For this task consistent analysis of suicidal thoughts, of sexual behavior, and of fantasies, all in the context of the transference, is essential. It is unnecessary at this juncture to describe more exactly or more fully the sequence of understanding and interpretation that is referred to by the words "consistent analysis," since that will be the subject of Chapter 2. What is to the point for the moment is to emphasize the importance of recognizing the complexity of the nature and origins of the psychic conflicts that give rise to suicidal thoughts and behavior.

It is equally important to keep in mind one's analytic knowledge of symptom formation and to apply it when one is analyzing patients with feelings of unreality or patients who complain chiefly about their actions, about their inability to be happy or content in the world in which they live, whether with respect to their sexual lives, their work, or ordinary social intercourse. It is uncommon for feelings of unreality to occupy a major position among the symptoms of patients in analysis, although there are exceptions (e.g., Freud, 1918; Rosen, 1955; Arlow, 1969a, 1969b). Since such feelings are usually relatively unimportant in the patients one analyzes, it is often not of great importance whether one is consistent in applying to them one's understanding of the relation they bear to psychic conflict, i.e., it is often unimportant whether one attempts to analyze them as one should. On the other hand, patients who complain of serious difficulties in social, sexual, and vocational relationships are very common in analytic practice, so it is often of great importance that an analyst be consistent in his approach to these aspects of a patient's behavior—important enough to justify some discussion of the matter.

A mistake that is commonly made with such patients is to contrast "normal" or "realistic" behavior and "defensive" behavior. It cannot be emphasized too strongly that such contrasts are never justified by the facts. It is never a case of "either-or." It is always a matter of "both-and." All behavior represents a compromise formation among the forces within the mind, a compromise that is multiply determined and one in which id, ego, and super-ego all play a part. This is, by the way, an illustration of the application of the principle of multiple function to clinical phenomena (Waelder, 1930; Stein, 1953; Brenner, 1959). Behavior is always in part instinctually gratifying, in part determined by defense against the very wishes it gratifies, in part self-punitive or penitential, and in part determined by external circumstances. It is never only one or another of these, though the importance of each may be very different in different instances and the practical needs of the moment may dictate that only one or only a few of the determinants be interpreted to a patient at a particular time. Even when this is so, however, the analyst himself must keep in mind that the full dimension of the patient's psychic situation includes the large number of factors just outlined and the analyst, at least, must remain responsive to evidence in his patient's associations concerning whichever of those factors remain to be discovered.

Some aspects of the difference between what is important *analytically* about a patient's behavior and what is not rarely cause practical difficulty, while others are more likely to do so. For example, Freud (1916, 1924) long ago called attention to the fact that some people go through life taking revenge on whoever is available for the injury or deprivation they are convinced they suffered in infancy, while there are others who are always on the lookout to be injured or taken advantage of. The former he called "the exceptions," the latter, moral masochists. It is seldom, therefore, that an analyst fails to recognize that there are psychic conflicts, in large part unconscious ones, that play an important role in determining the behavior of such patients and their attitude to the people and events about them. Even so, though, it is not rare for analysts to neglect some aspects of the underlying conflicts in favor of others. Thus moral masochism has been variously understood as a compromise between triumph and submission ("victory through defeat"), as a defense against loneliness or abandonment, as a way in fantasy of winning a sadistic parent's love, and as a derivative of a wish, derived from sadomasochistic primal-scene fantasies, to be loved by one's father. None of these explanations is false, but each is wrong in the sense of being incomplete (for a fuller discussion of this point see Brenner, 1959). It should be added that the importance of each as a determinant of a patient's behavior varies from patient to patient and that when such a patient is in analysis his analyst can decide which are the most important for that patient only by analyzing, i.e., by listening, by observing, and by interpreting.

But it is with respect to everyday aspects of behavior that the temptation to be inconsistent about applying one's analytic understanding is likely to be greatest. As was noted earlier, one frequently sees the attempt being made to decide whether this or that bit of behavior is "realistic" or whether it is "neurotic," when in fact the question is wrongly phrased to begin with. If, for example, a patient is physically ill, one's concern as an analyst should not be to try to decide whether he reacts "normally" or not, but rather to try to discover from his behavior and his associations what the determinants of his reaction are. To be sure, if a patient is forever running to the doctor for trivial symptoms or if, contrariwise, he refuses ever to see a doctor for even the most severe symptoms, we have no doubt that there are strong motives at work. But our interest as analysts should be to learn what the motives are, whether a patient's behavior in reaction to physical illness is as unusual as in the cases just cited or whether it is thoroughly conventional, for which read "normal."

The same holds true for object loss. "Mourning" is not the same for everyone, nor is there a uniform norm by which to judge it (Brenner, 1974a). What is important in analysis is to understand as thoroughly as possible what are the psychic conflicts that determine the particular features of the reaction of the particular patient in question to the loss of an object. Freud (1917a) concluded that the work of mourning consists in summoning up to the mind the many memories connected with a lost object and bidding each of them goodbye, as it were. It is, indeed, common for a bereaved person to be preoccupied with thoughts and memories of someone he loved who has just died, and it was doubtless this commonplace fact that served as a basis for Freud's conclusion about the nature of mourning in general. Clinical experience, however, indicates that the commonplace phenomenon just described can be both different psychologically from the simple decathexis of memories of a lost object and more complexly motivated as well.

For example, during the year after her father's death, a female patient dreamt of him several times in a very painful way: she was watching him as he sat or lay on his deathbed. His death had not been unexpected. It had resulted from pulmonary carcinoma, and his terminal illness had lasted a year, spanning the fourth and fifth years of the patient's analysis. Consequently there had been many occasions for her to learn more about her fateful and ambivalent relation with the dying man. Each of the dreams in question occurred on an occasion when the patient was angry at her father in retrospect, when something had just occurred to make her think, "The son of a bitch, I'm glad he's dead!" To dream of him was to deny this guilt-laden thought, though the wish-fulfilling aspect of the dream is obvious also. After all, she dreamt of him dying. The dreams were, in fact, typical compromise formations: conscious horror, sorrow, love, and compassion at the thought of his death; unconscious hatred and the joy of revenge.

Feelings and thoughts such as these about one who has just died are more than most persons can bear. They must be warded off, they must be defended against as effectively as possible. One way in which this is commonly done is to emphasize one's sorrow and one's love for the person who has died by dwelling in a painful, suffering way on memories of him. At the same time, this sort of preoccupation with reminiscences serves to deny the fact of death and to gratify libidinal wishes, often in an undisguised way. It is no wonder that it is so common for bereaved persons to react in this way during the period of mourning. The reaction seems likely to be much more than something that serves the purpose of detaching libido from the memories of the person who has just died, however. As in the case just cited, it seems rather that such reminiscences are daydreams that are not essentially different from any other fantasies. They are compromise formations, created according to the principle of multiple function, i.e., with many diverse determinants, among which their defensive function is prominent.

Similar considerations should guide one with reference to a patient's fears. One tries as a matter of course to discover what psychic conflicts are involved in a patient's fear of a realistically "harmless" situation, like an elevator or a crowded bus. But in analysis one should take the same approach to anxiety aroused in any other way as well, for example, by a truly accidental occurrence, like a vehicular accident in which the patient played no active part. It's not important that "anyone" would be frightened by such an event, that real danger was present and that anxiety is therefore "normal." What is important is to maintain an analytic attitude in all circumstances as far as possible. To do so is neither to "ignore reality" nor to brand a particular reaction, or the lack of it, as "neurotic." Thus, for example, on one occasion the suicidal, self-defeating patient mentioned earlier was involved in a freak accident. As he was driving on a city street a heavy object, perhaps a brick, fell from the upper floor of a building and struck his car, denting the roof badly. The noise was loud and disconcerting, but as soon as he realized what had happened he was quite calm, got the necessary information for insurance purposes and, to his own surprise, was quite cheerful about the whole affair. When he spoke about it in his analytic session later that day he added jokingly, "So you see, I'm not paranoid. They are really persecuting me." As he talked further it was apparent that one reason why he welcomed the accident and was pleased that it had happened was that it helped strengthen his defense of denial against awareness of his self-destructive tendencies. This time he could *prove* he wasn't responsible for his near demise. It seems likely that other determinants of his reaction were operative as well, e.g., unconscious gratification of feminine wishes, but what was most important in his associations and most useful to point out to him at the time was the way in which his accident reassured him and thus diminished his anxiety rather than increasing it.

Fantasies, hobbies, artistic and other interests, all "normal" by any reasonable definition of that term, should likewise be approached with what we have defined as an analytic attitude, since the fact is that each may be determined in large or small measure by factors that are as much a part of important psychic conflicts as are the symptoms from which the patient suffers.

For example, a patient had an interest in the history of his native city, an interest that had begun when he was a boy. At that time he had read everything he could find on the subject, particularly what it must have been like to live in the peaceful, lovely, unsettled area that was now all built up and full of people. If it were only like that still, or if he could only have lived in that earlier, happier time! This patient was the third of four children born two to three years apart. The oldest, a boy, was antagonistic to the patient and tyrannized him both verbally and physically. The youngest, a girl, monopolized their mother's attention when she was born. The patient's wish to live in an earlier time expressed his wish to be the old one in the family (father or older brother), to have his mother all to himself, free of all his rivals (the beautiful, uncrowded countryside), and for there to be no frightening jealousy or fighting (peaceful and lovely). His oedipal conflicts determined his interest in local history quite as much as they did his neurotic symptoms.

Another patient had a great love of the out-of-doors. She always enjoyed being in the country, whether farm land or woods and mountains. No food was tastier. than the berries she picked or the wintergreen or sour grass she chewed as she walked in the woods and fields. Like the patient just mentioned, she too disliked crowds. She avoided popular vacation spots. She preferred the countryside to be "just for her." In the course of analysis it was possible to date with certainty the patient's first visit to the country. It occurred during the summer before the birth of her sister. Since the patient was the oldest child in the family, she was at that time an only child and had her mother all to herself, as she never did again. Her jealousy of her siblings, her wish to have her mother all to herself, her anger at her mother for her faithlessness were all determinants of the patient's love of mother nature. The details of her love were determined by her particular conflicts and their childhood origins in the same way as were the details of her symptomatology, or of a dream or a fantasy. Its persistence and intensity in adult life reflected the persistence and intensity of the conflict itself.

It must not be supposed that I am recommending that special interests or hobbies of the sort just mentioned are to receive special attention or scrutiny in the course of analysis. On the contrary, what is recommended is merely that *whatever* a patient reports or does should be viewed in the same way, i.e., in the light of the analyst's understanding of the nature, the origins, and the consequences of conflict in psychic life. Again it should be noted that the question of the relation between an analyst's conjecture or understanding and the interpretations by which he conveys his understanding to his patient will be discussed in Chapter 2. The point here is that the consistent application of an understanding of psychic conflict is an essential part of a proper analytic attitude. It is a major determinant of the analyst's contribution to the analytic situation and thus to the analytic process itself. Moreover, when one has identified this feature of the analytic attitude and when one has an appreciation of its importance, one is in a better position to evaluate other recommendations that one sometimes finds in the literature or that one may have occasion to hear from colleagues concerning the proper attitude for an analyst to have. For example, Fenichel (1941, p. 74) was convinced of the value of behaving "naturally" with one's patients, and recommended that the "patient should always be able to rely upon the 'humanness' " of his analyst. True enough, but only within the limitations imposed by the analytic situation. Behaving naturally *as an analyst* is often a very different matter from behaving naturally as a friend, an adviser, a parent, or even as a good doctor in the ordinary meaning of the term. It is perfectly true, as Greenson (1967, pp. 190ff. and *passim*) and others have emphasized, that an analyst is a therapist, that psychoanalysis is a therapeutic procedure, and that the psychoanalytic situation is a therapeutic situation. What must be added is that therapist, procedure, and situation are all special of their kind. It is natural for an analyst to suggest to his patient that he tell his thoughts about having asked a question — even a "simple, practical" question about his analyst's schedule, for instance — rather than answering the question and being done with it if the analyst believes it likely, or even possible, that important unconscious motives played a part in the patient's having asked just that question at just that time. It is natural in the sense that it follows naturally from an analyst's knowledge of the effects of psychic conflict on thought and behavior and from his interest in learning as much as he can from his patient's thoughts and behavior about the nature and origins of the conflicts that motivate them, an interest that derives from and is justified by the analyst's expectation that such knowledge is necessary, or at least helpful, in achieving a favorable therapeutic result.

It is likewise natural for an analyst in the U.S.A. or in Britain not to shake hands with a patient at the beginning and end of each hour. Should he offer to do so he would be introducing into the analytic situation an unnecessary and hence an unwelcome psychic stimulus. By the same token, if an analyst on the continent did *not* shake hands, he would be introducing an unnecessary and therefore an unwelcome stimulus. The difference in behavior depends simply on the analyst's understanding of the difference between the meaning of his behavior (shaking hands) to a British or American patient and to a European one.

The same test should be applied to other ordinary social amenities. Just as a daily handshake implies more than civility and conventional politeness in some countries, so do expressions of sympathy and of good wishes. If such an expression means little to a patient at a particular time, little harm is done by proffering it. If it means very much to a patient, as sometimes it does, and if it is proffered without the patient's attention being directed to the value of his talking about his desire for it, his reaction to it, or both, the result may be disadvantageous to the course of the analysis. One should add, however, that it is just as unanalytic for an analyst to fail to pay attention to a patient's reaction to the fact that his analyst did *not* sympathize with him or wish him well as it is to fail to pay attention to a patient's reaction to an expression of sympathy or good wishes. What is most important in either case is an analyst's attitude of interest in the determinants of a patient's thoughts and behavior. Whatever one says or does as an analyst should be subordinated as much as possible to that attitude or be a consequence of it.

It is not possible, for example, to say to a patient, "Let's put analysis aside for a moment..." and proceed to advise him about some practical matter in his life, to ask his opinion concerning something of which he has expert knowledge, or to discuss a matter of mutual interest. Any such behavior must necessarily influence the transference and if an analyst deliberately excludes that influence from examination by pretending it doesn't exist, that "it's not part of the analysis," he has rendered the determinants of the patient's transference unintelligible to a greater or less extent. The extent to which he has done so will depend on the degree of relevance to a patient's wishes and conflicts of his analyst's "nonanalytic" intervention. If the relevance is great, the undesirable effect on analysis will be correspondingly great; if the relevance is small, the effect may not be of any practical significance. The difficulty is that one cannot always tell in advance whether the relevance of such an intervention is great or small. In any case, it is undesirable in principle.

The situation is different if something happens that is accidental, in the sense that it happens without the analyst's intervention. Such an occurrence, whatever it may be, has quite a different relevance to a patient's wishes and conflicts. The consequences in a patient's psychic life of what seem on the surface to be two identical events are very different if the one event was planned or encouraged by his analyst while the other was not. Thus, if he meets a patient by chance outside his office, an analyst should "naturally" behave in a conventionally appropriate way even though the same behavior would not be "natural," i.e., analytically appropriate, when both are in the analyst's office. What is even more important, however, is that an analyst's attitude toward any such event should be an analytic one—that he should be concerned primarily to understand from the patient's reaction to the event, and from his thoughts about it, as much as possible of the nature and origins of the psychic conflicts which determined that reaction and those thoughts to a greater or lesser degree.

The reader may have noticed that the preceding discussion has gradually become a discussion of the importance of maintaining a proper analytic attitude in dealing with the transference. Since a later chapter will be devoted to the subject of the transference, we shall reserve further discussion of such instances for that chapter.

SUMMARY

1. An essential part of an analyst's task is to understand the nature and origins of his patients' pathogenic mental conflicts.

2. A consistent focus on this task is, therefore, a major element of a proper analytic attitude. As far as possible it should determine an analyst's behavior in the analytic situation.

3. To be consistent in this regard one must keep in mind what the elements of conflict are, what function it serves, and what consequences it has in mental life.

4. When a symptom is accompanied by anxiety, both are consequences of the same conflict. *Symptoms do not produce anxiety.*

5. Symptoms, fantasies, dreams, behavior, in fact, all the elements of conscious mental life are multiply determined. They represent a compromise among id, superego, and ego. They are never attributable solely to drive, solely to defense, solely to environmental influence, or solely to penitential or self-punitive tendencies.

6. It is rare for an analyst to be inconsistent in applying this knowledge of psychic conflict to the analysis of neurotic symptoms or of familiar neurotic character disturbances. It is less rare for inconsistencies to appear in connection with the analysis of "psychotic" symptoms and of "normal" elements of a patient's character.

7. Being "natural," or, for that matter, being therapeutic or compassionate as an analyst means something different from being a sociable, friendly, sympathetic

"good doctor" or "good parent." It means acting toward one's patients in accordance with one's obligation to them, an obligation of which the first step is to understand the nature and origins of their pathogenic conflicts. It means, in other words, being guided by one's knowledge of such conflicts in general and by one's devotion to the task of learning as much as possible about one's patients' conflicts in particular.

2

CONJECTURE AND INTERPRETATION

We have seen in the preceding chapter that an essential part of the analytic situation is the analyst's attitude, i.e., his orientation to the task of discovering the nature and origins of each patient's psychic conflicts. We understand that the reason for this orientation is fundamentally a therapeutic one. As an analyst learns about his patient's conflict he conveys his knowledge to his patient with the expectation that his doing so will alter the conflicts in such a way that the symptoms they have caused will improve or disappear.

What an analyst says to a patient in order to inform him, in the broadest sense, about his conflicts is generally called an interpretation. The same word is often used as well to mean an analyst's own knowledge of his patient's mental life and conflicts. Analysts speak of "formulating an interpretation" or "arriving at an interpretation" when "interpretation" clearly refers to their own understanding of the determinants of a patient's mental functioning and not to what they have, as yet, said to the patient about those determinants. In most cases the ambiguity is unimportant, but for the purpose of this discussion the word "interpretation" will refer to what an analyst tells his patient about his psychic conflicts, while the word "conjecture" will be used to refer to an analyst's formulation in his own mind of what he has learned about a patient's psychic conflicts. It should be noted that, when used in this sense, "conjecture" says nothing about an analyst's sense of conviction that what he has learned is correct. It includes both what he is certain about and what he is uncertain about—both what he has long since decided must be so and what he has only just begun to suspect may be so. It should be noted that this definition is somewhat different from colloquial usage, according to which "conjecture" implies uncertainty. In deference to the colloquial connotation there will be times in the pages that follow when "understanding" or "conclusions" will be substituted for "conjecture" to refer to a conjecture that is strongly enough supported as to seem to be quite certainly correct.

Psychoanalytic articles on the formation of conjecture are few. One reason for this is that it is impossible at the present time to give a satisfactory general answer to the question, "How does an analyst know, or how can he guess with assurance at, the nature and origins of a patient's conflicts?" There is general agreement that one essential prerequisite is that an analyst must have been analyzed well enough himself so that his own conflicts neither blind him to those of the patient he is analyzing nor cause him to see the same conflict in every patient. It is for this reason that a personal analysis is a necessary part of every analyst's training. With each analytic case, however, the clues that guide one in forming a conjecture concerning that patient's conflicts are so many, so varied, and often so separated from one another in time that only one's personal experience as an analyst affords one any sort of satisfactory knowledge of the process of forming a conjecture and of the nature of the problems involved in doing so. The most one can do in a discussion like this one is to offer some comments on the subject.

It is interesting to observe how differently different analysts describe the process of forming a conjecture. It is clearly a process that is, at least subjectively, very different for different analysts. There are analysts who describe their conscious experience as entirely intuitive in this regard. Each conjecture comes like an inspiration, with no conscious thoughts leading up to it: "As I listened to the patient I realized that..." These analysts would agree with Freud's (1912b) formulation that as an analyst listens to his patient's associations, his unconscious mind receives impressions from the unconscious mind of his patient and can "reconstruct the patient's unconscious." Thus Isaacs (1939) wrote that a conjecture "is of the nature of a perception" and Isakower and Malcove (Malcove, 1975) expressed a similar view, while Reik (1937) added to this a warning that conscious, logical thought is positively detrimental to analytic perception. At the other extreme are analysts like Fenichel (1941), who described and illustrated the logical and intellectual aspect of conjecture formation. Fenichel emphasized the value of preliminary dynamic and genetic conjectures and sketched for his readers the process of progressive evolution and refinement of an analyst's conjectures as analysis proceeds, an

evolution that finally enables an analyst both to reconstruct the course of development of a patient's conflicts
and symptoms during the years before analysis began and
to explain their re-enactment in the transference as well
as their gradual alteration by interpretation in the course
of analysis. Thus, according to Fenichel, an analyst constantly revises his conjectures on the basis of new information as an analysis unfolds.

Other analysts have called attention to the value of
an analyst's paying attention to his own fantasies and
affective states as clues in reaching a conjecture concerning the determinants of a patient's associations or behavior. If, for example, instead of following what a patient is saying with his usual interest, an analyst finds
himself bored, he should ask himself whether this is because the patient unconsciously wants to bore him. It may
be, these analysts have pointed out, that this conjecture is
correct, and the same may be true if one finds oneself
irritated, provoked, sexually aroused, sleepy, or the like.
On other occasions one may become aware of a fantasy or
daydream of one's own as one listens to a patient (Beres
and Arlow, 1974), and its content may furnish a clue that
permits one to make a correct conjecture about the patient.

Intuition, conscious reflection, unconsciously motivated affective reactions or fantasies—all are potential
methods of forming a correct and useful conjecture about
a patient in analysis. There are analysts who are especially enthusiastic about one method or the other, but the
fact is that it makes little difference which method an
analyst uses if it leads him to the desired result. Most
analysts have probably used them all at one time or

another. Special preferences are doubtless determined by an analyst's own psychic conflicts. They are of interest to him as part of his own analysis, perhaps, but unless they interfere with his analytic work they have no other practical significance. They constitute an element of what one might call an analyst's professional style.

Conjectures, then, are the hypotheses that an analyst develops, whether consciously or unconsciously, to explain the nature and origin of the conflicts that determine what he has learned of his patient's mental functioning and mental development. They are an analyst's explanation of why a patient is the sort of person he is and why he behaves and talks as he does, both during his analytic sessions, when his analyst can observe him directly, and in his life outside his analyst's office, about which an analyst can learn only from the patient's account of it. Since conjectures are the conscious products of an analyst's mental functioning they must, like any other conscious products, be a compromise among the various forces or tendencies that are operative in the analyst's mind. They are determined on the one hand by external stimuli, which in this case are the patient's associations and behavior, and on the other hand by the interaction among id, ego, and superego derivatives and trends of the analyst himself. To avoid possible misunderstanding it should be repeated that in .this respect there is nothing unusual, nothing special about analytic conjectures. All our understanding of the world about us is the same amalgam of selective perception (Arlow, 1969a), wishful striving, and the conflicts that that striving generates. In the case of analytic conjectures this aspect of an analyst's mental functioning is usually referred to by such terms as empathy and introspection, and perhaps it would be in order at this point to say a few words on those subjects as they refer to the topic in hand.

Kohut (1959) proposed to distinguish analysis from other natural sciences on the basis that in analysis introspection plays both an essential and a limiting role, something that is not true, he maintained, in other sciences. In fact, however, empathy or introspection plays the same role in every science (Brenner, 1968b). One can never see the world without the participation of one's own wishes and conflicts nor without "empathically" personifying it. The very words we use attest that this is so. Force, energy, work, motion, are all words that derive originally from personal, subjective experience. Stones and planets aren't forceful or energetic. They don't work or even move actively and purposefully. These are ideas and words that describe ourselves and how we feel ourselves to be. The first physicists applied them to inanimate objects. In order for them to be usefully applied in that way, the terms had then to be redefined and depersonalized. More precisely, it was necessary in the development of physics as a science to take into account the fact that, contrary to our first natural, empathic assumption, the objects of the world about us that are not people behave in most ways very differently from the ways in which people behave. It took a very long time for physicists to learn this fully, though by now it is a lesson so well learned as no longer to be even thought of consciously. Psychoanalysts, however, are in a better position than physicists in this respect. Psychoanalysts are studying the mental functioning of other people, people who are, in fact, very much like themselves. They are, therefore, not in danger of being led astray by unconscious, subjective factors as badly as if they were to be "empathic" about molecules or planets. Still, there is some danger of being led astray in a similar way. However much people resemble one another psychologically they are different from one another as well, and it is important that the differences be recognized in psychoanalytic treatment. It is true that all patients are alike in that they all suffer from the effects of conflicts resulting from childhood instinctual wishes, conflicts which in every case involve anxiety, guilt, defense, self-punishment, and compromise formation. But it is equally true that the conflicts that result from instinctual wishes are never exactly the same in any two patients and that they are often quite different. More important, the differences are decisive in psychoanalytic therapy. Insofar as the aim of psychoanalysis is self-knowledge, all analysts agree that it is himself that each patient must learn to know, not what he has in common with the rest of mankind.

It follows then that psychoanalysts, like other scientists, must have some way of putting their conjectures to the test. They must have some means of deciding whether a conjecture is valid or not, whether they have guessed correctly about a patient or whether their conjecture must be revised, expanded, or even abandoned in favor of a different conjecture.

Some analysts recommend that in testing a conjecture, no less than in forming it, one should rely entirely on unconscious mental processes. According to them, if one has been well analyzed oneself and is "in tune" with one's patient's unconscious mental processes, the fact that one becomes aware of a conjecture is sufficient proof of its correctness (Baranger and Baranger, 1966; de Mijolla and Shentoub, 1973). According to analysts who support this view, what happens in analysis is what they call a reciprocal projective identification on the part of the analyst and patient that ensures the accuracy of the analyst's conjectures. They assert, therefore, that an analyst's knowledge of a patient's mind is qualitatively different from other knowledge and is not to be judged or tested by the same standards. Riviere (1936) likewise wrote, "We know that no psychoanalytic laws and facts can be proved in any written form."

At the other extreme stands the view of Kubie (1952) that psychoanalytic conjectures (and interpretations), being subjective rather than objective, can never be validated and are, therefore, scientifically untrustworthy by their very nature.

Perhaps both of these extreme positions are due in part to some misunderstanding of what the word "proof" really means in the field of science. Proof of a psychoanalytic conjecture, like proof of any hypothesis, theory, or law in natural science, means accumulation of supporting evidence. It is simply not in the nature of things for there to be "absolute proof" or "logical proof" of any proposition of natural science in the same sense that there can be proof for a mathematical proposition. A mathematical proposition can be logically proved or disproved because it is simply a statement of what does (or does not) logically follow from arbitrarily fixed premises known as postulates. Every proposition in mathematics has the logical form: "If A is so, then B must be so also." Scientific hypotheses are different from mathematical propositions in their very nature. They are basically empirical, not merely logical. They must agree with observed fact. They conform to no such uniform grammatical structure as do mathematical propositions and they are always subject to being discarded or revised in the light of subsequent experience. They are, to be sure, usually logically related to one another, but they are never merely logical inferences from a fixed premise. In science, logic is always subordinate to empirical fact, to the data of observation. The hypotheses, laws, and theories — in a word, the generalizations — of any science are, in fact, the best guesses we can make at the moment to explain the data with which we are presented.

How can all this be applied to the problem of testing psychoanalytic conjectures? One possibility, as noted above, is simply to rely on intuition. Those who do so either imply or say explicitly that one can rely on one's intuition with complete confidence in the result, that it is a method that cannot fail if it is properly used. Now if the intuitive conjectures of all analysts concerning the same material were in substantial agreement, this would at least lend support to the idea of relying wholly on intuition for the purpose of testing a conjecture. Even this support is lacking, however. An analyst's intuition often gives rise to conjectures that "do not appear convincing to all analysts in the light of their own experience" (Waelder, 1939, section II), to which we may add, or of the experience of those who taught them analysis. In other words, intuition, as Isaacs (1939) noted, is very much influenced by what one has learned, even though subjectively it appears to be "a direct perception." The fact that an analyst has reached a conjecture intuitively does not guarantee its correctness. It very often is correct, but the fact that it was reached intuitively is not sufficient proof that it is so. Validating evidence must be sought elsewhere.

The evidence that is most often used to validate a conjecture and that has the broadest range of possibilities for doing so is that which derives from a patient's response to a conjecture when it is put to him as an interpretation by his analyst. Even if it has not been put to him as an interpretation, however, a patient may confirm a conjecture by what he says (and does) spontaneously after the conjecture has been formulated. For example, the suicidal patient who was mentioned in the previous chapter behaved, at a certain stage of his analysis, differently on Monday and Tuesday than he did later in the week. It was my conjecture that this was so because he missed me over the weekend. Before I interpreted this to him, though, I waited a couple of weeks for confirmation of my conjecture by repetition of his behavior. Only after this was forthcoming was an interpretation of his behavior offered to him.

This sort of confirmation might be described as repetition of the evidence on which the conjecture was based in the first place. It would make little difference to the course of analysis whether such a conjecture is consciously formed now or a week or two from now. In some cases evidence confirmatory of a conjecture may turn up in a patient's associations only after months or years. In one case, for example, a young man's competitive activities, vocational as well as avocational, were severely inhibited by fears of being humiliated by his opponents or competitors both verbally and physically. It was not till after this had been interpreted to him many times with many different examples, however, that the conjecture that he feared castration in particular was confirmed by a memory from late adolescence. He remembered thinking to himself at that age that he could probably be a superlatively successful student if his balls were cut off so that sexual wishes and masturbation didn't interrupt him when he wanted to study.

Another kind of validating evidence for a conjecture can be provided by prediction. For example, in the case of the suicidal patient mentioned above, his fear of his unconscious affectionate, sexual, and murderous wishes for me was so great that, on the basis of past experience, it would be safe to predict that he would no longer show the same signs during his Monday and Tuesday hours of having missed me over the weekend after his attention had been called to this feature of his behavior. One could predict that he would have to prove me wrong, partly in order to defend himself against his ambivalent transference wishes and partly to gratify them. When this turned out to be the case, therefore, it provided confirmatory evidence for the conjectures that had been formed about the anxiety those wishes could produce.

Another example of how a conjecture may be confirmed or validated by a patient's subsequent associations and behavior is the following. A young woman of 26 announced after a summer holiday that just after the start of the holiday she had begun again to see her old boy-friend, F., a man 20 years older than herself who had been recently widowed and who already had a steady girl-friend. She declared herself ever so happy and content. She had not missed me a bit and was not a bit jealous of F.'s other girl-friend. In fact, she never thought about her at all and was not in the least dissatisfied with F. for spending so little time with her. One day she said, "F. stayed last night after we made love longer than he ever did before. It was so good." Since "longer than he ever did before" meant more than ten minutes, I interpreted to her on the following day that she was hiding from herself her hurt, her jealousy, her loneliness, and her anger at F. for treating her as he did. She listened to what I said with no response other than a half-hearted, but pleasant, statement of disagreement. The next day, however, she was in a bad mood and proceeded to quarrel with me about the fact that I would not cancel her hour on the following day, when her dog had to be taken to the vet, and spoke of stopping analysis at the end of the month. How could she trust such a hard-hearted person as me to be a good analyst? Besides, she had never been convinced that analysis could help her anyway, etc., etc.

My conjecture was that the important immediate reason for her being angry at me and wishing to leave me was the interpretation I had made the day before about her being hurt by F.'s inattentiveness and angry at him for it. Since she was clearly in no mood to consider even the possibility that her conscious hostility to me had any grounds other than the rigidity of my schedule and her distrust of analysis as a form of treatment, I said nothing to her about my conjecture. A week passed, at the end of which she came in one day and admitted she had cried the night before and that her crying "had to do with F.," but insisted nonetheless that she wasn't really upset by not having heard from him and that she was now all over her tears and felt quite cheerful. Once again I told her that she was hiding from herself her hurt, jealousy, loneliness, and anger at F. This time she became furious, shouted at me, "Stop! I warn you! Stop saying that!" and, as I finished, yelled, "Now I suppose you're happy that I'm angry and expressing it!" with which she ran out of the room, slamming the door behind her. Not a very welcome confirmation of my conjecture of the week before, but certainly a dramatic and convincing one.

The explanatory, or heuristic, value of a conjecture may also afford evidence of its correctness. Freud (1923b) mentioned that the best proof of the accuracy of an analytic reconstruction is that it represents the only way to fit together all the pieces of a patient's life, just as there is only one way to fit together all the pieces of a jigsaw puzzle. It may be worth observing that this sort of validating evidence involves a kind of implicit statistical analysis of a very pragmatic sort (see Schmidl, 1955). It is a way of expressing the idea that, on the basis of what we know from our experience with life, the probability of there being two or more reconstructions that would explain *all* the known facts about a patient is so small as to be negligible, even though it cannot be precisely calculated.

Finally, it occasionally happens that a conjecture can be confirmed by an extra-analytic source of information: the testimony of another person, a photograph, a diary, etc. (see Bonaparte, 1945). Welcome as such confirmatory evidence is when it appears, it appears so rarely that its practical value is usually slight when compared with evidence that derives from the analytic situation itself. Conjectures derive essentially from analytic material in the first place and are, in the great majority of instances, either confirmed or contradicted by that material. Waelder (1939) suggested as an ideal in this regard that an analyst, in listening to his patients, should "look at facts until they seem to speak for themselves."

When all is said about conjectures that can be said, however, both as to how they are arrived at and how they can be either supported or contradicted, the fact is that in one's work as an analyst conjecture is but a first step in the vast majority of cases. The second is to convey conjecture to the patient, i.e., to interpret, and so close is the connection between the two that, as we have seen, but one word is often used to refer to both.

Much has been written about interpretation and interpretations, and the contributions that have been made to the subject vary from those that deal with very general considerations to ones that focus on very particular and even individual points. There are articles on when to interpret and how to interpret, about interpretation and affect, about tact in interpretation and about proper timing, about the order of interpretations—defense before content—about deep interpretation, about interpretation upward, about including the transference in an interpretation or not, about interpretation and resistance, about the importance of precision, of avoiding analytic terms and of using the patient's own vocabulary, and about the different meanings an interpretation can have to a patient and its consequent multiple effect, including some that are nearly independent of what one has said and that depend rather on the patient's realization that one has listened and responded. Despite the great interest and value that such articles possess, however, they are all, by and large, instructive chiefly as adjuncts to one's own clinical experience. If read in the absence of such experience they will nearly all seem to be either trite or unintelligible. One learns such things mainly from experience with patients and from discussing one's experience with supervisors and colleagues. No attempt will be made, therefore, to review these many contributions critically, nor even to summarize them.

Instead, some general comments will be offered about the subject of interpretation which the reader should understand as being supplementary to what he has already heard and read rather than as replacing it or substituting for it.

It is worth repeating what it is that one hopes to accomplish by interpretation so that one has clearly in mind from the start what its role really is, or should be, in analysis. The principal purpose of interpretation is to convey to a patient what one has learned about *his* psychic conflicts. That isn't always the main thing that happens when one makes an interpretation and it is never the only thing that happens. The effect on a patient of a particular interpretation is never limited to increasing his knowledge of his own conflicts and in some cases an increase in knowledge is only a small part of the effect an interpretation makes—its chief effect may be that the patient feels discovered, accused, humiliated, praised, encouraged, rewarded, seduced, or rejected. Nevertheless, the intended effect is to increase a patient's knowledge of himself, and even if one's every single effort in that direction is not successful, the sum of one's efforts—the net effect of one's many interpretations—must be successful if there is to be any analysis worthy of the name. To assert (or imagine) that there is a "process" of analysis that is essentially independent of interpretation in this sense of the word is a contradiction in terms. "To analyze" can only mean to help a patient to know himself better. Any other form of psychotherapy is not analysis. It may be equally successful therapeutically in a particular case. It may be even more successful than analysis in some cases, but it is not psychoanalysis.

Experience has shown that much time is needed for anyone to learn much about wishes and fantasies that he has all his life struggled to ward off because of their potential for anxiety and guilt. One of the lessons that every analyst learns early is that, contrary to the expectation that most of us have when we begin with our first analytic patient, interpretation is a gradual, oft-repeated process: that one says the same thing to a patient in many ways and on many occasions before it has its full effect. If variety is the spice of life, surely repetition is an essential ingredient of analytic interpretation, nor is very long or profound reflection necessary to explain why this is so. Analytic interpretations of any importance concern powerful motives and equally powerful defenses against them that have deeply influenced a patient's thought and behavior for a lifetime and that have involved him in ceaseless conflict—conflict that he could not control unaided. No wonder, then, that a single interpretation, however precise, inclusive, well phrased, and well timed cannot produce a permanent beneficial alteration. No wonder that its effect is a relatively brief one and that much repetition of it is needed before a patient truly understands himself differently and better than he did before. The patient himself may be nearly unaware of the whole long process or he may remember only the last of the many interpretations made to him on a given subject and may think of the change in himself as produced on that one occasion. The analyst knows that it was in fact produced only by long and persistent analytic work that involved not one but many interpretations to the same effect. The adage that small causes do not produce great effects applies to psychoanalytic interpretations. When one reads a clinical example in which a single interpretation seems to have resulted in a striking change in a patient one is justified in assuming that much preparatory work had preceded it and that it was far from the first interpretation of its kind.

An appreciation of the fact that important interpretations can exert their full effect only gradually and after many repetitions helps one to realize that no single interpretation is ever likely to be as important for the successful conduct of an analysis as is one's general plan for one's interpretive work with a patient. With rare exceptions it is not this or that interpretation that counts as much as the cumulative effect of many interpretations, all reflecting a correct conjecture—in more familiar terms, a correct understanding—concerning the nature and origin of a patient's relevant conflicts. An analyst should certainly attempt to formulate every interpretation he makes as precisely as possible, to pick out just the aspect of the patient's childhood conflicts that is active at the moment so that he can best relate the present to the past, but an analyst can also be secure in the knowledge that if he is pretty much on the right track with a patient, if he understands him pretty well, i.e., if his conjectures about the relation between past and present are reasonably correct, any interpretation he makes is likely to be helpful in furthering a patient's knowledge of himself, even if it is not the very best and most precise interpretation that could be made. On the mark is best, but close to the mark is still good, and unless one's conjectures about a patient are wrong or very deficient, one is likely to be close enough.

It should be added that correct interpretations do not only promote a patient's insight. They also lead progressively to a fuller and more accurate knowledge on the

part of the analyst. As every analyst knows, correct interpretations are generally followed by "fresh" analytic material, i.e., by memories, dreams, fantasies, symptoms, or
transference reactions that both confirm an analyst's conjectures to date and shed fresh light on the subject as well,
thus permitting him to correct or amplify his conjectures.
Such responses to interpretations on the part of a patient
have been described by a number of authors (Brenner, in
Panel, 1955; Fenichel, 1941; Freud, 1937; Hermann,
1933, pp. 99-104; Isaacs, 1939; Reik, 1937) in papers
which were concerned, for the most part, with criteria for
validation of interpretations. They are usually explain-
able as resulting from diminution of anxiety (and guilt),
relaxation of defenses, and greater tolerance of instinctual derivatives, and one usually anticipates a concomi-
tant amelioration of symptoms.

It has been observed both by the authors just mentioned and by others (Kris, 1947; Schmideberg, 1949)
that symptomatic improvement is an unreliable index of
the efficacy and correctness of interpretations, and this
for two reasons. First, there may be a paradoxical worsen-
ing of symptoms, a so-called negative therapeutic reaction (Freud, 1923a, p. 49); and second, a symptomatic
improvement may result from other than analytic reasons, e.g., from an unconscious wish to avoid further
analysis—the so-called flight into health—from the beneficial effects of a positive transference, or from a change
in a patient's life situation, whether for better or worse,
since for some patients a "real" calamity such a sickness,
injury, loss of a loved one, etc., can cause a temporary
disappearance of their psychogenic symptoms instead of
exacerbating them, as more often happens. Nevertheless,
despite the unreliability of symptomatic improvement

alone as an index of the correctness of one's conjectures, it is an indispensable part of the confirmatory evidence. One can hardly claim to have understood and treated a case correctly in the absence of any symptomatic improvement. The presence of such improvement is not, by itself, conclusive proof that one has done so. Its continued absence, however, strongly suggests that one has not.

Other confirmatory reactions to a correct interpretation, correctly phrased and timed, have been listed by several of the authors cited above. No attempt will be made to draw up a complete list here. They include such things as recognition with surprise ("You know, I *never* would have thought of that!"), a feeling of familiarity ("Of course. That's something I've always known without realizing it."), the return of a forgotten memory, a confirmatory dream in the next day or two, an affective reaction such as tears, guilt, rage, or laughter, confirmatory associations, a slip, confirmatory action ("acting out"), and so on. As Fenichel (1941) observed, they can all be included under the general heading of evidence that a patient's conflict has been substantially altered in the direction of diminution of defense and the emergence of clearer, more direct derivatives of the frightening, guilt-laden impulses being warded off, whether those impulses are instinctual derivatives, self-punitive impulses of the sort Freud (1923a) described in connection with what he called negative therapeutic reactions, or some combination of the two.

It is worth noting that most of the descriptions of reactions confirmatory of interpretations deal with a single interpretation. This is understandable, because such reactions can be illustrated most conveniently by a vignette of manageable length. Nevertheless, as has been noted above, such descriptions and illustrations tend to be misleading, since from them the reader may get the mistaken impression that it is single interpretations that are crucially important, rather than the long sequence of interpretations, all based on a single conjecture or, at any rate, on a closely related group of conjectures, that is in fact of greatest importance in the vast majority of analyses. The following brief report may perhaps serve to illustrate the point.

The patient is a man who entered analysis two years ago at the age of 40. Of crucial importance in his childhood history is the fact that he was twice separated from his family. On the first occasion, at the age of four, he was sent to the country for three weeks when his brother was born. A year later he developed scarlet fever with bilateral otitis media and was treated in a hospital for two months. During his hospital stay he was operated on several times. The patient himself had never attributed great importance to either of these experiences. He had no memories of the first and only the slightest of memories of the second—an image of his parents' faces separated from him by a pane of glass. Nor did it seem likely to him even after I had raised the possibility that they could be in any way responsible for the unhappy feeling, of which he complained when he began analysis, that his life was unsatisfying, bleak, and loveless. On the contrary, he consciously agreed with his wife's insistence that the disharmony in their marriage was a result of inadequacies in his own character and he hoped to be able to overcome the defect in his character with the help of analysis. He accused himself of being negligent of his wife and children and indifferent to them and of having married his wife for her money because he feared he couldn't make a living "on his own." He was on a friendly, though not unusually close footing with his mother and brother. His father had died six years before the patient began analysis. It is of some interest that the only time the patient could remember weeping as a grown man was after he had returned home from the hospital to which he had gone to collect his father's possessions after the latter's death.

It soon became apparent that this patient rarely expressed anger at anyone except himself. When someone offended or injured him he customarily blamed himself for the incident and felt ashamed of being so inadequate and incompetent as to have provoked it. He also blamed himself for his lack of affection for people who had hurt him in one way or another—for his "coldness" toward them. During the course of several months this pattern of inhibition and self-recrimination was often interpreted to him in connection with whatever example of it he happened to have brought at the time. Sometimes such an interpretation would be followed during the hour by a more direct expression of angry feelings at whatever person he was talking about at the moment, sometimes by increased awareness a day or two later of the persistent anger he felt at his wife or business partner, and sometimes by evidence, usually indirect, that he was angry at me for "encouraging" him to express his anger instead of helping him to keep the peace. Finally, after several months, he recalled one day that when he was in junior high school he had been falsely accused of responsibility for a disturbance in the auditorium and had been grilled and threatened for hours in the principal's office to get him to confess to what in fact he hadn't done. He finally confessed "just to get out of there." He remembered thinking at the time, "Tell them they're right so they'll stop it already and let you go."

The recovery of this memory was obviously confirmatory of the repeated interpretations that he was afraid to be angry or to complain, and that he blamed himself instead. As such it was welcome, but it did more than merely confirm that line of interpretation. In addition it offered support for the conjecture, as yet uninterpreted to the patient, that his hospital experience when he was five was an important reason for his inability to complain or to be angry, since what he remembered thinking when he was in the principal's office in junior high school sounds so like what a hospitalized five-year-old might be told: "If you want to get well fast and go home soon, do what the doctors and nurses tell you to do. If you fight or disobey, you'll just have to stay longer." Besides, as every five-year-old knows or quickly learns, it's useless to fight the doctors and nurses. They're so much bigger, so much stronger, they can always make you submit if you don't give in and agree on your own. If you give in, the nurses praise and pet you. If you don't, they don't love you as much and in the end you have to do what they want anyway.

To repeat, this example illustrates the point that it is not a single interpretation that produces progress in analysis—in this case, recovery of an important memory that opened the way to further understanding and interpretation. Progress results rather from a sequence of interpretations based on a single conjecture or on a group of related conjectures. In some cases analytic work goes more quickly, in others more slowly, to be sure. But whether it be quicker or slower, the psychological changes brought about by a line of interpretation that deals with an important aspect of a patient's conflict come only bit by bit and always over an extended period of time.

Since interpretation is an essential of the analytic process, it will be referred to frequently in the chapters to follow, either explicitly or implicitly. Such references belong more naturally in the context of later chapters, however, than they do in this one and they will therefore be reserved for their more natural place in our exposition. Before proceeding to the next chapter, however, we may summarize the contents of this one as follows:

SUMMARY

1. We have distinguished conjecture or understanding in analysis from interpretation in order to simplify and clarify our discussion of these two aspects of an analyst's activity.

2. Different analysts prefer, or prefer to emphasize different methods of forming conjectures, e.g., intuition, conscious reflection, unconsciously motivated affective reactions, and unconsciously motivated fantasies. Such preferences seem to be elements of an analyst's professional style. Any or all of these methods can lead to a useful, correct conjecture.

3. An analytic conjecture is a compromise formation in which various elements of an analyst's own psychic conflicts necessarily play a part. The same is true, however, for conjectures or hypotheses in every branch of empirical science. In particular, the roles that introspection and empathy play in the formation of an analytic conjecture (hypothesis) are not substantially different from the roles they play in generating other scientific hypotheses.

4. In the empirical sciences the word "proof" can refer only to the presence of validating (confirmatory) evidence and "disproof" to the opposite.

5. In analysis, the most common and the most reliable form of validating evidence derives from a patient's response to an interpretation based on the conjecture whose validity is to be tested. Evidence may come from other sources, however, some of which are described and illustrated.

6. Symptomatic improvement is a necessary criterion, though not in itself a sufficient one, for validation of a line of interpretation and the conjecture(s) on which it is based.

7. Intepretations can and do have multiple effects in analysis. The effect that is intended and that is, therefore, common to all interpretations is to produce an alteration in a patient's psychic conflicts that permits the emergence of progressively less distorted derivatives of the components of his conflicts.

8. This change is the essence of the psychoanalytic process.

9. It is necessarily slow and gradual.

10. It depends on the cumulative effect of many repeated interpretations that reflect an analyst's correct conjecture(s) — conjecture(s) that are repeatedly tested, refined, and enlarged as analysis proceeds.

11. No single interpretation, however precise and well timed, is likely to produce a great and lasting effect. Any single interpretation, therefore, is less important than is a consistent line of interpretation that is based on a correct understanding of or conjecture concerning a patient's conflicts.

3

DEFENSE ANALYSIS

Defense analysis is a subject that has occupied the attention of analysts since shortly after the publication of "Inhibitions, Symptoms and Anxiety" (Freud, 1926). The pioneer books on the subject are *The Ego and the Mechanisms of Defense* (A. Freud, 1936) and *Problems of Psychoanalytic Technique* (Fenichel, 1941). Since their publication the topic has never ceased to be of interest to analysts, to judge from the number of articles devoted to it. In fact, if one were pressed to pick a single characteristic of modern psychoanalytic technique that could serve to distinguish it from the stages that preceded it, one could do no better than to point to the analysis of defenses. Without it, analysis is essentially id analysis, as indeed it was in the beginning (Kris, 1951). With it, analysis came to include ego analysis as well. As Waelder (Panel, 1967) put it, whereas in the 1920's analysts conceived their task to be to discover all the hidden fixation points of each patient's libido in order to free it from its fixations, analysts today are no longer concerned only with a patient's repressed infantile wishes, i.e., with his fixations, they are also concerned with the anxieties to which those wishes give rise and with the means that are used to defend against them.

Among the recommendations in the literature concerning the technique of defense analysis is the dictum that defenses should be analyzed before one analyzes the instinctual derivatives they ward off or oppose (Fenichel, 1941, p. 45). This recommendation is usually understood as an example of the general principle of interpreting or analyzing what is on the surface, psychologically speaking, before analyzing the depths, since defenses are thought of as being more superficial and more accessible to a patient's awareness than are the wishes that they oppose.

There are, certainly, many instances in which this recommendation applies. It is obvious, for example, that if a patient is bending every effort to remain unaware that he is so angry that he wants to kill everyone in the whole world, it makes no sense to tell him that he is a murderer at heart. At best, he won't believe it. At worst, he'll either become very upset or leave treatment altogether. Still, the question arises whether what one actually does in the analysis of such a patient is to interpret his defenses before saying anything about the instinctual derivatives they oppose. Let us consider as an example that should help us to answer this question, the interpretations made to the patient described at the end of Chapter 2.

It will be recalled that this patient regularly blamed himself and was angry with himself in order to avoid knowing he was angry at someone who had offended him.

In addition, he was constantly ready with such platitudes as "It's always easy to blame the other fellow," and "Nothing was ever accomplished by losing your temper." As noted in the preceding chapter, the conjecture (understanding) that he was defending against or warding off his anger in these various ways was repeatedly conveyed to him in interpretations during a period of several months. Here is clearly a case of defense analysis. But were the interpretations limited to the defenses he used? Not at all. They included references to the instinctual derivative being warded off, namely, to his anger, as well as to the defenses against his anger. In each interpretation something was said that referred to his being angry at someone he knew for something that person had done or failed to do. The main emphasis in each interpretation may have been, at least in my mind, on the fact that the patient was blaming and criticizing himself in order to divert his attention from his critical and angry thoughts about someone other than himself, but the fact is that each interpretation contained some reference to the drive derivative being warded off as well as to the defense employed for the purpose. It would be incorrect, therefore, to say that the defense was interpreted before the drive derivative. Both were interpreted at the same time. To be sure, it would be a technical error in such a case to interpret only the drive derivative and to neglect the defense against it, but it would be no better to interpret only the defense, without reference to what was being warded off.

The same sequence of interpretations illustrates a further point, namely, the inclusion of genetic interpretations along with dynamic ones. In this case the genetic interpretations were based in part on a recovered memory and in part on reconstructions. It will be recalled that after several months the patient remembered a pertinent event — he remembered being grilled for hours in the office of his junior high school principal about a disturbance in the auditorium that he was wrongly suspected of being responsible for, and he remembered confessing guilt, at last, "just to get out of there." This memory, as was noted earlier, helped in the understanding of the origins of his particular means of defense. That is, it suggested and supported certain conjectures concerning the importance of his experiences in the hospital when he was five years old that were outlined in Chapter 2 and that need not be repeated here.

Shortly after remembering his experience in the principal's office, the patient began to be aware of an element of another aspect of his conflict, the content of his anxiety. As this new material emerged in the course of his associations, it too was included in my interpretations. To be explicit, he realized that he was afraid that if he showed his anger he would be rejected and unloved. "Who wants someone around who's angry all the time?" was the way he put it.

For some time, though, this was an idea that he expressed without too much conviction that it meant very much to him. Gradually, however, as he became more and more able to admit to himself his long-standing dissatisfaction with his wife and some of his criticisms of her, he began to really feel lonely, unloved, unhappy, and as though life was passing by without him and there was nothing he could do about it. He even wondered whether life was worth living after all, since it brought him so much misery and so little happiness. He was dissatisfied with analysis and with me, though for the most part he expressed his dissatisfaction as self-criticism. At times he was more direct, however. One day, when he felt very discouraged, he asked, "What does it matter what happened to me when I was four? It's my life *now* that I have to do something about! It's how I feel now that counts. That's what concerns me.... I don't know whether this is the right form of treatment for me.... What do I want you to do? I don't know. I guess, to give me an injection of antibiotic and make me all well."

The reader will remember that the reason for the patient's hospitalization and subsequent operations when he was five years old was scarlet fever—a bacterial infection. When he suffered from it, antibiotics were not yet available. Had they been, neither the hospitalization nor the operations would have been necessary. In fact, within a few years after the introduction of antibiotics, the hospital was closed because it was no longer of use. I may add further that the last time I had mentioned his hospitalization to him had been ten days before the associations just given. What I had said at that time had apparently stayed in his mind without his having talked about it since.

To return to the exposition, one may say that, taken all together, these reactions and associations appear to furnish additional support to the conjecture that his hospital experiences at the age of five and his separation from his parents when he was four contributed importantly to shaping the precise nature of his conflict and the particular content of his anxiety. They certainly demonstrate both his longing for love (instinctual derivative) and the danger associated with it (loneliness and despair).

Thus this simple example of analytic work in progress, though it is neither profound nor unusual, can serve to illustrate what the analysis of conflict actually is in practice. An analyst does not interpret in a schematic way from defense to drive derivative, from present to past, nor even from less important to more important. On the contrary, he is guided in his interpretations, in the first place, by the understanding he has gained already of the nature and origin of his patient's conflicts, i.e., by his conjectures, and, in the second, by the order in which relevant new or confirmatory information appears in the patient's associations. Defense, drive, anxiety, guilt, and compromise formations, both in their current operations and in their historical development, are all interpreted either alone or in combination with one another as they appear in the patient's associations, and not according to some schematic formula. They are interpreted in whatever order and in whatever way seems most likely to further the analytic task of helping a patient to understand himself better in the analytic meaning of that term, i.e., of helping him to become more adult and less infantile — among other things, less afraid and less guilty — in the face of his own wishes. To speak of defense analysis as though it were something separate and apart from the analysis of the other elements of psychic conflict is, in fact, to run the risk of misleading both oneself and one's listener. Defense analysis, like id analysis and superego analysis, is a part of the analysis of conflict and compromise formation, whether the compromise under scrutiny is a symptom, a dream, a fantasy, a character trait, or a parapraxis. Whatever one is attempting to analyze, one must necessarily pay attention to the defense(s) that have played a part in its genesis, but one never does so in an isolated way.

What has been discussed so far has been principally the question of the order of interpretation in analytic work with particular reference to the analysis of defenses. There is another question that has been discussed by many analysts on different occasions (De Saussure, 1954; Hoffer, 1954; Loewenstein, 1954; Weiss, 1967; Panels, 1954, 1970, and 1972). Put most succinctly, the question is this: "What happens to a defense when a symptom has been analyzed?" Or, to put it at somewhat greater length, "What are the changes in particular defenses or in patterns of defense that result from the successful analysis of a patient's symptoms or characterological difficulties? How do defenses change in the course of psychoanalysis?"

Here again I shall refer to a clinical example in order to illustrate my answer and to document the reasons for it.[1] The patient was a 29-year-old woman who had been in analysis for six years at the time of the episode to be reported. The relevant data concerning her preanalytic and analytic history are these. Prior to analysis she had had sexual relations only with women. Her behavior during these affairs was dominated by her unconscious need to deny (1) sexual feelings for her father, (2) jealous and hostile wishes toward her mother and her older, married sister, and (3) her rage and humiliation that she did not herself have a penis. Thus, for example, when having sex with a woman, she had the fantasy, which was unconscious prior to analysis, that she herself had a penis, that she was a man in a sexual embrace with a woman.

In the course of the analysis, the patient had sexual intercourse with men for the first time. During inter-

[1] The example that follows is taken from Brenner (1975b).

course she sometimes had conscious fantasies of controlling her partner's penis. At other times she imagined that his penis was part of her body rather than of his. These heterosexual affairs were interspersed with homosexual ones, each of which was initiated by her unconscious need to defend herself against sexual longings for her analyst. These she warded off by assuming the male role in a homosexual relationship, just as, before analysis, she had warded off her unconscious sexual wishes for her father.

At the time with which we are concerned, the patient was once more involved in a homosexual relationship. It had begun some months before, just after her analyst had left for his vacation. Though consciously struggling to give up her current girl-friend, she was obviously resentful of her analyst and was trying to provoke him. She complained with righteous indignation that he behaved unfairly toward her and that he never gave her her due. During one session, when she was arguing with herself that she should give up her girl-friend, she paused frequently, obviously waiting for her analyst to speak. He finally did intervene to say that she was trying to get him to order her to give up her girl-friend so that she could rebel, as she had so often tried to get her parents to take a position she could use as an excuse for rebelling against them. He did not add to this interpretation in words what the patient well understood because it had been interpreted to her many times in the past on appropriate occasions, namely, that her anger at her parents throughout her life and at her analyst now was really because she hadn't been given a penis and because neither her father nor her analyst loved her as she was sure they would have if she had really been the boy her father had hoped for before she was born. Thus this interpretation, as the patient understood it, had to do with the patient's wish for love and for a penis in the transference situation and with the fact that it was the frustration of those wishes that made her feel toward her analyst the anger that she attributed to him, via projection, lest she feel guilty, i.e., to avoid superego condemnation.

On the occasion just described, this interpretation appeared to have a considerable effect upon the patient. During the next week she showed the following changes:

1. She discontinued the homosexual affair.
2. She was more feminine in dress and manner.
3. She began to date a man.
4. She asked an older, male colleague, an obvious father figure, to accept her as a pupil, even though she was "sure" he'd refuse.
5. She was much less angry at her analyst and was aware that she wished to be close to him.
6. She had a frightening dream, the associations to which led to thoughts of being sexually excited while on her analyst's couch. It should be noted that she did not actually feel sexually excited either in connection with those thoughts or at any other time when she was on the couch.
7. She became aware of being angry at her mother, at her older sister (a lifelong rival), and at a married female friend.
8. She recalled feeling that she had longed to be close to her father when she was five years old.

Here is a situation, then, where as a result of an interpretive intervention considerable changes occurred in a patient's symptoms, in her associations, in her dream life, and in her behavior. To be sure, the effective interpretation was not made for the first time on the occasion just described. On the contrary. It had been made many times previously in one form or another. Still, this time it was followed by substantial changes in the patient's mental functioning, and it seems, all things considered, suitable for our present purpose, which is to answer the question, "How do defenses change in the course of psychoanalysis?"

What then were the changes that the interpretation just described produced in this patient's defenses?

The reader will recall that before the interpretation the patient was not conscious of love and sexual longing for her analyst. Instead, she was angry at him. In other words, her loving and sexual wishes were defended against (warded off) by a reaction formation in which hate or anger replaced love. Her jealous and angry wishes toward women whom she saw as rivals were also dealt with by reaction formation. She was not conscious of negative feelings toward such women. Instead, she was carrying on a love affair with a girl for whom she yearned, and by whom she was sexually aroused.

Her castrative and vengeful wishes toward men were dealt with in a different way. She felt mistreated by her analyst—shortchanged by him. In other words, she projected her anger onto him. Still another defense involved in her unconscious effort to deal with her castrative and vengeful wishes toward men was identification. She played the part of a man in the sexual affair she was having.

Finally, the memories of her feelings of longing for closeness with her father when she was five had long since succumbed to repression, a repression which lifted only after the interpretation was made.

We can say, therefore, that before the interpretation in question the patient was using repression, reaction formation, projection, and identification as defenses against certain of her instinctual derivatives and superego demands. It was these defenses that were affected by the interpretation her analyst made to her. How were they changed by it?

First of all, the patient's pattern of reaction formations changed. That is, she gave up her homosexual affair and began dating men. She also expressed anger at female rivals on several occasions—her mother, her older sister, and her married friend—while she was less angry at her analyst than she had been and was aware of wishing to be close to him. In other words, the reaction formations of love for women in order to ward off anger at them and of anger at men in order to ward off love for them were both much diminished.

Second, repression of some memories of her oedipal wishes for her father were undone. At the same time we may safely assume that many other related memories remained repressed. That is, repression was diminished rather than wholly undone.

Third, identification with the older, admired colleague who was her new teacher clearly played a role in her becoming his pupil.

Fourth, isolation of affect was apparent in the ideas she expressed of becoming sexually excited on her analyst's couch. It will be recalled that the patient expressed these ideas in the course of associating to an anxiety dream.

Fifth and last, the mechanism of displacement apparently played a role in her anger at her married friend, since it was evident at the time she expressed her anger that she was really angry with her mother and that her friend was a substitute target.

Thus we can say that after the interpretation the patient's defenses included repression, identification, isolation of affect, and displacement.

If we attempt now to itemize the defensive changes that occurred as a result of the interpretation made to the patient, we come up with the following conclusions:

1. Identification with men persisted, though with significant changes that will be discussed below.
2. Castrative wishes were repressed after the interpretation instead of being projected, as they had previously been.
3. Reaction formation against heterosexual wishes was much diminished and was in part replaced by isolation of affect.
4. Reaction formation against hatred of mother and sister was also diminished and was, in part, replaced by displacement.
5. There was partial lifting of repression of oedipal wishes and memories.

How can one generalize about these changes in defense? Can one say that pathogenic defenses disappeared, or that they were replaced by normal ones, or even that more infantile defenses were replaced by less infantile ones? None of these formulations seems justified by the data of observation.

For example, a defensive identification with men was present both before and after the interpretation. Before the interpretation this identification decisively influenced her sexual behavior. She had wooed a woman and was engaged in a sexual relationship with her, a relationship in which the patient played the part of a man. After the interpretation the same identification was expressed in her vocational behavior. She took steps to become the pupil of a man she admired in order to learn his skills and to be able to use the tools of his profession — tools, it may be added, that had for her a phallic significance. In other words, both before and after the interpretation certain aspects of her behavior were motivated by identification with a man, an identification that served to defend against her feminine, oedipal wishes. (That it also gratified her masculine wishes is true but irrelevant to our present discussion.) That there was a significant change in her behavior no one can doubt. She became more mature — more normal one might fairly say. Before the interpretation, her masculine identification was expressed in a homosexual affair. Afterward, it was expressed in her relationship to an older man, her teacher, whom she proposed to emulate vocationally in a realistically rewarding, socially desirable way. But what of the defense of identification itself? She still identified with a man. The tools of her teacher's profession were transparently phallic symbols and to learn to use them certainly expressed her unconscious fantasy that she had a penis. Can one honestly say that her use of identification as a defense was any less infantile or more "normal" after the interpretation than before, even though the behavioral pattern — the compromise formation — that included it must be rated more mature as a whole?

If one turns to the defense of reaction formation, one is faced with similar difficulties. This defense, to be sure, diminished. It did not persist essentially unchanged as did identification. But it was replaced, at least in part, by isolation of affect and by displacement. Can one say that these defenses are less pathogenic than is reaction formation, or even that they are less infantile, less regressive? Or consider the defense of repression. Clearly repression was lifted in one respect following the interpretation. Certain oedipal memories from the age of five years emerged for the first time. Yet repression intensified in another respect, since the patient's castrative wishes toward her analyst were repressed after the interpretation, whereas they had been warded off by projection before it. In this case, then, projection disappeared after the interpretation, it is true, but repression, a potentially pathogenic defense by any standard, appeared in its place.

I believe that there is but one way out of this seeming impasse. One cannot, I think, generalize about the changes in defenses which result from psychoanalysis as long as one concentrates on each defense by itself, isolated from the conflict as a whole. One must think, not of defenses as such, but of the entire conflict of which they are a part. To illustrate, one can sum up the consequences that the interpretation in question had upon the patient's defenses in the case we have been discussing rather simply by saying that after the interpretation the patient was better able to tolerate conscious awareness of a number of derivatives of her positive oedipal wishes than she had been before the interpretation. In other words, her defenses against them were less intense after the interpretation than before it. The derivatives referred to can be listed as:

1. Affection for her analyst.
2. Longing for his love.
3. Memories of affection and longing for her father's love when she was a child.
4. The wish to be closely associated with an older, admired man and to be his pupil.
5. The wish to attract men and to have sexual intercourse with them.
6. Anger at rival women.

To put the same idea in different words, what happened was that it was no longer necessary after the interpretation for the patient to defend against certain of her instinctual derivatives in order to avoid anxiety and guilt. Before the interpretation those particular derivatives could not be tolerated. They were too frightening or too guilt provoking. After the interpretation they could be tolerated. Before the interpretation she had reacted to them in ways that we classify as defensive. That is, her yearning for love and sexual gratification from an older man (father, analyst, teacher), together with the associated jealousy of older married women (mother, sister, friend), were represented in conscious thought and behavior as a desire to rebel against such men, to castrate and supplant them, and to spite them, while being on loving terms with women. After the interpretation her reactions to the same wishes and jealousy were less defensive, in the sense that the resulting compromise between drive derivative and defense allowed more in the way of gratification. The change was not so complete that no defenses were necessary. Quite the contrary. The patient's reactions to her positive oedipal wishes after the interpretation were no less a compromise between defense and drive derivative than they had been before. What are often called pathogenic defenses against oedipal derivatives were as easily identifiable after the interpretation as they had been before it. Even though the new compromise formation was different in important respects from the previous one, it was still a compromise formation for all that.

It seems, then, that one cannot speak of alteration of defenses in isolation from conflict and compromise formation as a whole any more than one can speak of the analysis of defenses as something separate and apart from the analysis of the other elements of conflict. Whatever example one chooses from an actual case, one is forced to the same conclusion. It is true that not all changes resulting from defense analysis are as easy to present in concise form as the one just given. More often than not the changes that occur in the course of analysis following any one interpretation are slighter than in our example, so that one has about them an impression of gradual change and one cannot easily document the relation between interpretation and psychological change without presenting analytic data that cover a period of several weeks or months, something likely to tax the patience of the reader no less than the power of the analyst. Regardless of the ease or difficulty of presentation, however, the conclusion must be the same in every case: it is the compromise formation that changes, not this or that defense. Defenses are never abolished as such, not even the "pathogenic" or "infantile" ones. Compromise formation is as much characteristic of mental functioning after successful psychoanalytic work as before it. It is the nature of the compromise that changes in the direction of mental health or normality, not the defenses per se.

As is always the case when a number of variables are involved in a final result, it is not easy to know to what degree each of the variables contributes to that result, or, to put it somewhat differently, how important each one is. Thus when a psychic conflict changes as a result of analysis, how much is this due to the fact that, once a patient knows what it is that has frightened him or made him guilty since childhood—once he is conscious of the content of his guilt and anxiety, i.e., of the nature of his childhood fears—it no longer frightens him so much, since he is now an adult and is no longer helpless when alone, just as he is no longer convinced of the real possibility of castration? Probably a good deal, but probably not entirely. One may reasonably suppose that other factors are involved as well. In the case we have discussed, for example, the patient had had a number of sexual experiences with men during the course of her analysis. Perhaps the instinctual gratification afforded by these and other experiences of a sort that she had never had before she began her analysis played a significant part in reducing the intensity of her conflict over her incestuous and castrative wishes. Strachey (1934) and others have pointed to the importance of still another factor, namely, to the diminution in the severity of superego demands and prohibitions during the course of analysis as a result of partial identification with one's analyst. Perhaps the relative importance of each of these factors varies from case to case, perhaps it is roughly the same in all, or in all with similar conflicts. All that one can actually observe with certainty is the change in the nature of the compromise formation. About the relative importance of the reasons for the change, one can, as yet, only speculate.

In addition the conclusions that we have drawn concerning the question whether defenses disappear or change during analysis serve to remind us that defenses are not, after all, a special class of mental functions. Since we usually think of defense in terms of defense mechanisms, i.e., in terms that do label defenses as a special class of mental phenomena, the statement that they are not a special class of mental functions deserves some explanation.

Defenses are mental phenomena that are definable in terms of their purpose or, if you prefer, in terms of their function, which is to prevent or to hinder the development of anxiety associated with instinctual wishes and self-punitive trends. It may be added parenthetically that the word "anxiety" should be replaced by the word "unpleasure," since, as we shall see in the next chapter, defenses also serve to hinder the development of depressive affects associated with the instinctual life of an individual and with his self-punitive tendencies. For the moment, however, we can leave aside this extension of our definition and limit the term "defense" to the purpose of avoiding anxiety that would otherwise result from instinctual wishes and/or self-punitive trends. The means that can be used to implement this purpose in one instance or another, i.e., the potential means of defense embrace the entire range of ego functions. For example, masochistic wishes may be prompted by the ego in order to avoid or minimize the anxiety associated with sadistic ones, and vice versa. Love, pity, and compassion can be similarly emphasized, as is often seen in reaction formation. One sees defensive displacements—sometimes regressive, sometimes not—from phallic wishes to oral or anal ones, as well as the reverse. Intellectual activity can serve the purpose of defense. So can an interest in social customs, in fashion, in political activities, sports, art, vocational pursuits, and so on. The defensive functions of emphasizing ethical and moral standards and practices are so obvious that one need only mention them. The fact is that, although the best-known defenses are those included in the familiar list of defense mechanisms (A. Freud, 1936; Brenner, 1973a, p. 87), no such list can be considered to be exhaustive. Everyone can, and at one time or another everyone does use whatever is available and useful for the purpose of opposing a frightening or guilt-laden wish in order to minimize the development of anxiety. Indeed the same ego functions that serve as executants of the drives, the same ones that promote instinctual gratification under one set of circumstances are used defensively at other times or, for that matter, simultaneously. There are no special ego functions that are "defenses," functions that serve solely a defensive purpose and no other. Ego functions are all-purpose, as it were. They mediate instinctual gratification, they are used to oppose instinctual derivatives, they serve as means of enforcing or opposing superego prohibitions and demands, and they enable one to adapt in the psychological sense of the word to one's environment.

To put the matter succinctly, a defense is not a thing, it is a posture, specifically, a mental posture (see Brenner, 1975b). To ask, "What happens to defenses in analysis? Do they disappear? Do they go away?" is like asking, "What happens to your lap when you stand up?" "A lap" is not a thing any more than a defense is. Both are useful concepts that refer to a posture, the one to a physical posture, the other to a mental one. Thighs are thighs, whether they are vertical or horizontal. Their function, however, is (or can be) different, depending on their posture, and "a lap" refers to one of their possible functions when they are horizontal. The same is true for ego functions. When they serve one purpose, they are executants of drive derivatives. When they serve another, they are defenses against them.

SUMMARY

1. Although the term "defense analysis" is too firmly entrenched in the literature for there to be any likelihood of its being changed, it should be understood to mean "analysis of the defensive aspect of conflict." Defense analysis is not done and cannot be done in isolation, separately and apart from the other dynamic and genetic aspects of conflict.

2. As analysis proceeds, defenses change, but they neither disappear nor do they change in any uniform or even regular way. For example, they do not necessarily become less "pathogenic" or less "infantile."

3. Defenses are not special ego functions. The same ego functions serve drive gratification, defense, superego demands, and adaptation either alternately or simultaneously. Properly speaking, a defense can be identified only by the purpose or function it serves in the psychic economy of opposing (warding off) some psychic impulse or tendency. To identify it primarily by the method used to achieve its purpose, as is so often done, though it has the advantages of convenience and familiarity of usage, has the disadvantage of ambiguity and possible misunderstanding.

4

SUPEREGO ANALYSIS; AFFECTS AND PSYCHIC CONFLICT

When superego demands and prohibitions are allied with defenses against instinctual derivatives, superego analysis becomes essentially a part of defense analysis. As such it requires no special discussion. Whatever one has to say about defenses in general and about the anxieties they are intended to avoid applies equally well to superego demands and superego anxiety, i.e., to fear or expectation of punishment, self-reproach, or both.

The psychic situation is more complicated when self-punitive trends are themselves warded off or defended against, something to which Freud (1923a) called attention long ago as the mechanism of an unconscious sense of guilt. The following vignettes are illustrative (see Report, 1969).

In the course of the analysis of a woman in her thirties, the patient's mother was hospitalized for a meta-

static carcinoma. Her condition deteriorated progressively, and after a final week during which she lay in a coma,
she expired. The patient spent many hours by her mother's side, but, as it happened, she was not present at the
moment she died. For this she reproached herself bitterly
and repeatedly during the analytic sessions that followed
immediately on her mother's death. Over and over she
blamed herself for leaving her mother as she had done
and placed on herself the responsibility for her mother's
death. "If I'd only been there, I could have called a nurse
or a doctor and maybe saved her life," by which was
meant, prolonged it for a few hours or days.

Both by her extreme—one is tempted to say, self-
less—devotion before her mother died and by her self-
reproaches after she had done so, this patient justified the
conclusion or conjecture that she was guilty because of
unconscious wishes to kill her mother, wishes that had
their origin in early childhood. Of this, however, the
patient had no inkling. Her guilt was displaced from its
true source—her wishes that stemmed from the past—to
a falsely rationalized one, i.e., her actual behavior at the
time of her mother's death. For her guilt to be analyzed,
the defenses against it had to be undone and its true
source revealed.

In this instance superego analysis meant making the
patient aware that she had displaced her guilt from past
to present. Once the displacement ceased, analysis could
proceed. It is worth noting, however, that the patient's
extreme devotion to her hopelessly ill mother during the
weeks before the latter died was in part motivated by the
same need to defend herself against death wishes and the
guilt arising from them as were her self-reproaches after
her mother had died. Her behavior served unconsciously

as a way of establishing that she was innocent of responsibility for her mother's death. In the case of this patient, to be sure, her defenses, especially after her mother had died, proved to be inadequate to their purpose of avoiding guilt and self-reproach. They were, as is so often the case, but partially successful.

It may be noted in passing, however, that it is not rare for such defenses to be more successful than they were in the case just mentioned. The relatives of a dying person are often able to diminish very much the guilt they feel about his illness and death by a show of devotion, of attention, and of self-sacrificing behavior. That this fact is commonly, though not always consciously understood is suggested by the frequency with which relatives of a dying person are told, "Don't do anything now that you'll feel sorry for later," i.e., "It's worth being attentive and self-sacrificing now, because, if you are, you'll feel less guilty after whoever is sick has died."

Another mechanism for relieving guilt that is commonly used is projection. It is often the case that when a patient has died the surviving relatives vehemently, even irrationally, accuse the hospital, doctors, and nurses who cared for him of responsibility for his death. Those who make such accusations are not infrequently motivated to do so by a need to diminish or avoid the guilt that stems from their own unconscious wishes about the dead person by thus projecting them.

To return to our main topic, the following is another vignette to illustrate defense against guilt. It comes from the same source (Report, 1969) as did the first vignette. The patient was a married man of 30 whose rage at his mother was, as far as one could tell, entirely displaced to his wife, whom he continually reproached for neglecting him and with whom he fought bitterly. His conscious attitude toward his mother was one of pity for her inability to fulfill her obligations as wife and mother and of admiration for what he claimed was the fortitude with which she bore the burden of lifelong semi-invalidism. He was aware that his older brother made no secret of the fact that he considered their mother to be a pampered, self-centered malingerer, but this knowledge seemed to have no effect whatever on the patient's thoughts and feelings, which were reinforced by the firmly held moral dictum that one's mother is immune from criticism by the children she has born. "Honor thy mother," seemed to be the first commandment in this patient's moral code.

"Why was it imperative for this patient to ward off all hostility toward his mother?" is the obvious question, but the answer did not become clear until after considerable analytic work had been done. It then appeared, finally, that according to family tradition his mother's illness and incapacity had resulted from the patient's birth. He had, as he had heard repeatedly throughout his childhood, "nearly killed" his mother when he was born and he had reacted to this tradition with an intolerable sense of guilt as well as with great anger. His defenses of displacement of hostility from mother to wife and of filial piety as a moral obligation served the purpose of warding off not only his wish to tear his mother to pieces but also the guilty conviction that he had done so already with dreadful consequences both to his mother and to himself. In other words, they served to defend against his intolerable guilt.

As one can see from these examples, there are times when it is important to analyze a patient's conscious guilt feelings or feelings of moral obligation as an essential part

of the analytic work that is necessary to the proper understanding of the nature and origins of his pathogenic
conflicts. In the first case, what led to a better understanding of the patient's conflicts were not her conscious
self-reproaches but her unconscious ones. Consciously she
reproached herself for having shortened her mother's life
by having left her side for a few minutes, but this conscious self-reproach served mainly to ward off the true,
unconscious one, which was that she *wanted* her mother
dead. In the second case, it was neither naivete nor a
devotion to conventional morality that was responsible
for that fact that the patient clung so to his conscious
ideal of filial piety. The real explanation for the tenacity
with which he clung to his ideal was his unconscious need
to ward off the lifelong guilt connected with his rage at
his mother and with the conviction that he had torn her
apart by being born. Neither case could be properly
understood until the unconscious meaning and source of
certain conscious superego manifestations—self-reproaches and feelings of guilt in the one, an ethical ideal
in the other—were discovered.

An important part of what deserves to be called
superego analysis thus consists of dealing analytically with
defenses against superego derivatives and, in doing so,
improving both one's own understanding of the conflicts
of which those derivatives are a part and that of the
patient as well. But the problems posed in analysis by
superego functioning can be still more complicated than
those we have considered till now, as the following example will illustrate.

A young man in his early thirties, who had been in
analysis for three years, finally finished a report on which
he had been working for several weeks. It was a report

on a controversial matter and was necessarily critical of some past and present policies of the firm that employed him. Additionally he had set himself the task of improving his style of writing, which meant to him avoiding a tendency to write in a prolix, polysyllabic way and being simple, direct, and lucid instead.

He appeared for his hour the next morning unwashed, unshaved, and dressed in blue jeans, an old, soiled shirt, and a windbreaker. He had overslept, he explained, and had rushed out of the house at the last minute. What he had planned to do was to get up early so as to be in his office in time to edit the typed draft of his report, correct any mistakes it contained, have the typist prepare the final draft, and submit it to his superior by midmorning. As it was, he would have to return home to wash, to shave, and to dress, wouldn't even get to his office till midmorning and probably wouldn't be able to submit his report in time for his superior to have it over the weekend, as he had requested.

"So, fuck him! He'll have it Monday."

After some further discussion of the trouble he'd had with the typist, who was inexperienced and made many mistakes, the patient told of a visit with his father the evening before. In the course of their visit his father made a casual allusion to the obvious fact that the patient was stronger and in better physical shape than himself and was capable of greater physical effort. The patient realized more keenly than ever that his father, who had always seemed invincibly strong, had become a fat old man and really didn't have so many more years to live, and that he, the patient, was now the stronger of the two. He felt a surge of compassion and love for his father, but when the latter revealed that he had another engagement for dinner, the patient refused his invitation to be one of the party.

"Fuck him! Who needs him?" said the patient.

He then fell silent for a minute or two and began to think, as he later explained, "That bastard's been sitting there listening to me this whole time and hasn't said a word. Why doesn't he say something?"

He then looked at his watch to see if it was time for him to leave. As I cleared my throat, the patient said, "What's the matter? Did you decide to spoil you record?" i.e., spoil my record of silence.

Since both his wanting me to talk and his looking at his watch had come up before, I asked whether he had been wanting me to talk while he was silent and whether looking at his watch had been expressive of the thought, "If he (i.e., the analyst) isn't going to say anything, to hell with him! I'm leaving!"

"You get 'A'," the patient replied sarcastically.

It should be added that the patient had already told me that, after leaving his father the evening before, he had called a girl and gone to bed with her before going to the apartment of his regular girl-friend to spend the night with her.

Clearly such a complicated and dramatic sequence of events involving the patient's relation to his employer and colleagues, to his father, to his girl-friend, and to myself must have many determinants—far too many to hope to be able to unravel them in any brief presentation. For our present purpose, however, we can restrict ourselves to one of the many determinants, deliberately neglecting the others.

For some time before the session described above the patient had recurrently brought up the subject of the world being turned upside down, sometimes by other people, sometimes by his own actions. On one occasion he had a feeling as though everything were upside down when he was unexpectedly successful in his work. On another occasion it was when an important public figure was sent to jail. On still another, it was when he thought of the possibility of a colleague of mine trying to disprove one of my ideas, and, finally, he remembered a scene from a film in which a man wooed a girl by demonstrating his strength in acrobatics, which included standing and walking on his hands, something that, the patient added, he could never learn to do. "When I stand on my hands, I get all dizzy and sick to my stomach," he said.

As a consequence of my interpretations to him on these several occasions, the patient was already somewhat familiar with the idea that for him to be successful in competition meant unconsciously to triumph over his father both in physical combat and by winning his mother's love as well. He knew also, from interpretations made on many occasions, as well as from confirmatory memories of childhood events, dreams, daydreams, etc., that he had unconsciously avoided too great success in any directly competitive activity for two main reasons, first, his fear of his father, who was both very strong physically and very successful, even eminent, professionally and, second, his guilt at the thought of hurting, killing, or humiliating his father, for whom he felt great admiration and love as well as envy and hatred.

How is all of this to be understood from the admittedly restricted viewpoint of the patient's superego functioning? In part, it is understandable in terms of defenses against superego functioning of the sort described above. For example, he wanted to be reconciled with his father, which he had hoped to do by going out to dinner with him alone and then spending the evening together. The fact that it meant something special to him for his father to be loving him in this way he denied by thinking, "Fuck him! Who needs him? I've got other people who are glad to be with me!," meaning his girl-friends.

The self-punitive wish that his regular girl-friend be angry with him was also warded off by lying to her about having gone to bed with another woman. The wish that I treat him meanly, e.g., neglect him by remaining silent, as though he were a boy and I an adult, was warded off both by pretense of indifference — "To hell with him, I'm leaving!" — and by patronizing me — "You get 'A'."

There is another part of the patient's superego functioning, however, that cannot be understood either in terms of fear of punishment or of defense against it. What this part of his superego functioning involved was rather the patient's reactions of remorse and his wish for reconciliation. For the patient to complete his report symbolized for him the accomplishment of his unconscious wish: to turn the world upside down, to win his mother and to triumph over and destroy his father. Having achieved this goal symbolically, he reacted by behavior that expressed penitence and the wish to be forgiven. He dressed like an uncared-for adolescent, he arrived late for his hour, which not only made him feel rushed and harried, but was likely, he thought, to make me and his superior at work critical of him, he felt compassion for his poor old father, he felt me to be neglecting him, and, by his sexual behavior, he ran the risk of having his girl-friend get angry with him, should she discover his infidelity. It was consonant with this aspect of his motivation that when the recommendations in his report were accepted without opposition or even debate a few days later, what he expressed to me when he told me about it was principally disappointment. It was only after I called to his attention this evidence of his conflict over success that he was able to tell me that he had been exultant over his "victory," and that the disappointment, which he rationalized as due to having been deprived of an opportunity to debate with the opponents of his recommendations, had come only later.

At any rate, it's clear that having succeeded in his rivalry with me and his father, he unconsciously felt remorse and pity, belittled himself, looked for punishment, forgiveness, and love from his defeated rivals, and made a partial effort to be rejected by the woman who unconsciously represented his mother. Though it is neither unfamiliar nor unusual (Freud, 1919, 1924; Alexander, 1933; Klein, 1935), it is important to note that such a combination of superego derivatives involves something more than the usual formulation of defense against instinctual derivatives in order to prevent or minimize the development of anxiety. That formulation described quite accurately the patient's difficulty in writing his report in the first place. It took many weeks longer and far more effort to write than it would have taken were it not for the unconscious prohibitions and threats of punishment that opposed it. The same could be said for many previous attempts to succeed vocationally or otherwise, attempts that had for years been largely unsuccessful. All of these are understandable as a consequence of defense against instinctual derivatives to avoid anxiety. But when he succeeded in writing what he considered a good report in language as simple and direct as he felt my interpretations to him to be, he was no longer able to avoid anxiety and guilt by defending against his wishes. He had then to expiate his "bad" deed in various ways: by feeling unhappy, by degrading himself, by being punished in one way or another, by pitying and feeling protective toward his rival(s), by seeking their love, etc.

A reaction of this sort—what Klein (1935) and others call reparation—is a familiar type of superego derivative. Its very familiarity in clinical practice perhaps accounts for the fact that it is rarely thought of as deviating from the standard model of conflict: impulse, anxiety, defense against impulse, compromise formation. Yet it is clear that it does deviate from the model. To repent, to do penance, and to placate someone who is displeased or angry, however unconsciously all of these are done, is not quite the same as warding off an instinctual derivative lest one be blamed and punished for gratifying it. Consequences of superego activity of the sort illustrated by the example just given are among the manifestations of conflict that support the suggestion (Brenner, 1975a) that it is both appropriate and advantageous to view conflict in relation to unpleasure, of which anxiety is but one variety, rather than to view it, as has been usual since the publication of "Inhibitions, Symptoms and Anxiety" (Freud, 1926), exclusively in relation to anxiety.

To return to the example we have been considering, it seems to be related dynamically both to the cases that Freud (1916) spoke of as "wrecked by success" and to the phenomena that Alexander (1930) referred to as "corruptibility of the superego." In all of them some success is achieved that is unconsciously equated with gratification of a forbidden wish, but only on condition that punishment and penance can either precede or follow gratification.

There are patients whose entire lives have been lived under the shadow of an infantile success or gratification that has unconsciously made them guilty and that remains a source of conflict throughout their lives. Such patients' guilt, and the conflicts occasioned by it, are, as it were, one of the strands that has been woven into the fabric of their mental lives and that has played a decisive role in the final outcome of their infantile instinctual development.

Take, for example, the suicidal patient described in the first chapter. One unconscious reaction to his father's death when he was three, a reaction reinforced by the subsequent series of losses of father substitutes, was the fantasy that it was he, the patient, who had killed him. The guilt associated with this parricidal victory manifested itself in various ways throughout the patient's life. For one thing it probably contributed to the intensity of the patient's desire for a close and affectionate relationship with an older man, a desire that the patient recognized quite consciously and that he had no hesitation in attributing, in adult life, to the longing he had felt as a boy to have a real father of his own, as his friends did. But there was no doubt that it was responsible in large part for a feature of the patient's relationships with older men of which he was quite unaware, a feature that can be summarized as a need to provoke older men who were in positions of authority over him into being angry with him and interfering with his vocational advancement. The most dramatic example of this occurred some years before his analysis began. It was precipitated by a tragic accident: one of his superiors was murdered by a burglar, who shot him while rifling his apartment and then escaped. Like everyone else in his organization, the patient was shocked. Like many, he was personally grieved as well. A few days after the funeral he left work with no conscious plan or intention, went to a department store a short distance away, and got himself arrested for shoplifting. Fortunately for him, his friends in the organization in which he worked were successful in obtaining his release without charges being brought against him and the whole affair was hushed up on condition that he see a psychiatrist. This he did, but for a few weeks only, and without any real involvement in treatment. It was not until a few years later, after he had been in analysis for some time, that he realized that his superior's murder must have so intensified his chronic guilt at having, as he fantasied, got rid of his father (whose death had also been a violent one) that he was driven to pose as a robber in order to get himself arrested and punished. Usually his provocative behavior was far less dramatic than in the instance just described, but the unconscious need to atone for his fantasied responsibility for his father's (very real) death was an important part of his mental life right up to the beginning of his analysis, a part that was often seriously detrimental to his chances both of success and of happiness.

In other, similar cases it is the death or prolonged illness of a sibling that has given rise to the unconscious conviction of having done something that must be denied or atoned for throughout life. It may be added that not all the consequences of such a reaction are pathological. It is not rare, for example, for a physician to have been unconsciously motivated in his choice of profession by his need to heal the sibling for whose childhood death or illness he unconsciously feels responsible. One would not expect such a motive ever to be the only reason for becoming a physician, but it can sometimes be one of the important ones, perhaps even the decisive one, as in the case of a patient whose decision to specialize in pediatric cardiology was the result of her reaction to the fact that her younger brother had spent more than a year of his childhood in bed with rheumatic fever.

Here, then, are cases that illustrate an additional complication of superego analysis, namely, instances in which remorse and fear of punishment are related not to unfulfilled wishes and longings of instinctual origin but rather to the fulfillment and gratification of such wishes. Such cases cannot be understood in terms of danger and anxiety alone—in terms of fear of what is to come. Some of the unpleasure derives not from what is to come, but from what has already happened—from disappearance of a parent, loss of a loved sibling, etc. The ambivalence that is an inevitable characteristic of incestuous object relations tends to obscure the distinction between these two sources of unpleasure. It is easy to view affection and longing for a vanquished and hated rival as being nothing but a defense—one similar to reaction formation in that love and regret are used to ward off hatred and triumph. This formulation is doubtless true enough for practical purposes in many cases, but it is not so in all. The patient mentioned above, whose father met a violent death when the patient was in his fourth year, missed him bitterly many times thereafter. He yearned for a father to help him to be more manly, to protect him from his mother when she was angry, to earn money so that his mother could stay home instead of going out to work, so that she wouldn't have dates with other men, and to dissipate her frequently voiced fears of their all being hungry and homeless. The patient whose reaction to writing the report was described was also very fond of his father and reacted with hurt and anger throughout his childhood whenever he felt that his father paid him too little attention or showed him less affection than he did a sibling or other rival. For these patients, as for many others, grief over losing a parent, whether in fact or in fantasy, was not just a defensive reaction. It was a reaction to a real calamity as well.

Moreover, there are situations of psychic conflict in which one cannot attribute much if any role to anxiety, situations in which a patient's defensive reaction serves the purpose of avoiding or minimizing, not the unpleasure of anxiety, but unpleasure associated with what has already happened.

The most familiar instances of this kind are those that have to do with a little girl's reaction to the realization that she is different from boys in that she has no penis. One aspect of that reaction—one part of her penis envy—is the conviction that something terrible has happened to her. It is in this, incidentally, that the chief difference lies between the castration complex of girls and that of boys. In the former, the emphasis is more often on the idea that something bad—castration—has already happened, while in the latter, as has so often been noted, it is the prospect or danger of castration that receives the principal emphasis. The two examples that follow will serve to illustrate the former reaction, namely, that "something bad," i.e., castration, has happened. It must be born in mind, however, that this is not the only ideational content of what I have proposed to call depressive affect (Brenner, 1974b, 1975a). Object loss and loss of love may be equally well involved in depressive affect.

The first example is that of a woman in her early thirties who came to analysis primarily because she felt nothing but unhappiness in her current life, didn't see how she could ever be happy, and had never been able to form a lasting relationship with a man that brought her joy. One day she remarked in the course of her associations that she had not felt "comfortable with her body" for many years. This puzzling remark was explained by her associations: she dated the onset of her discomfort to her thirteenth year and her attempts to describe her discomfort made it clear that she had felt dissatisfied with her body since that time. From what she had told me earlier I knew her menarche had occurred when she was twelve. I knew also that she bitterly envied her younger brother, who bore their father's name, and that her unconscious wish to be a man was very strong, to judge from many aspects of her adult thought and behavior. It seemed justified, therefore, to explain her feeling of dissatisfaction with her body as a consequence of menarche. When she began to menstruate she felt forced to admit that she was really a girl—that she wasn't a boy after all, no matter how much she longed to be one. The result was that forever afterward she was dissatisfied with that body of hers that had so disappointed her by becoming a woman instead of a man. As it happened her persistent feeling of dissatisfaction never troubled her greatly. It was not prominent among her symptoms, so that it made little practical difference to her analysis whether that particular feature of her difficulties was understood and interpreted. Nevertheless, it clearly resulted from her unconscious reaction to unpleasure connected with something that had happened, rather than to anxiety, i.e., to an anticipation of unpleasure. When she first menstruated, it was for her a repetition of an earlier disappointment, the disappointment she had felt in early childhood when she compared her own body with that of her brother and was convinced that hers was defective because she had no penis and was, as she was convinced, inferior to her rival. Thus one of the many consequences of her feeling of inferiority was that she never felt "comfortable with her body" after she began to menstruate and to develop breasts.

Incidentally, the reader may note that this conscious feeling of discomfort was a compromise formation. It expressed her anger at being born a girl clearly enough, but at the same time it deflected her attention from "herself"—particularly from her genitals, which were now not only defective but bloody, i.e., damaged beyond hope of repair—to "her body." This defense of displacement must be rated as only a partially successful one, however, since a considerable degree of conscious unpleasure persisted.

The second example is the homosexual patient who was described at some length in the chapter on defense analysis. Among the determinants of her homosexuality was the conviction from very early in her life that if she had only been born a boy her father would have loved her best, a conviction that was strongly reinforced by his proposal that the family adopt a little boy when the patient was in her fifth year. What this meant to the patient in her early years was that being without a penis was a calamity that had befallen her. One of her reactions was a strong and persistent masculine identification that included the fantasy that she was really a boy after all, that she really had a penis. At the time she began analysis this fantasy was no longer conscious, but as analysis progressed she became aware that in her sexual affairs with women it was important for her to be assured, both by her partner and by herself, that the finger or tongue she used to stimulate and gratify her partner was "just like" a penis, or "just as good as" or "even better than" a penis. Thus one of the ways the patient used to avoid her feeling of intense unpleasure about being without a penis was to deny what she had felt all her life to be a defect, to pretend she was a man, and to imagine that she had a penis—in fact, a super one (see Rado, 1933).

The brevity of the two examples just given is unavoidable in any written presentation such as this. To present the full scope of the nature and consequences of penis envy plus convincing confirmatory analytic material would require more space and skill to present as well as more time to read than author and reader have at their disposal. To neutralize this difficulty as much as possible the examples chosen are what might be called commonplace ones. That is, they are reactions that are not unusual in themselves and that derive from the commonplace reaction of very young girls to the anatomical difference between the sexes, i.e., from penis envy. One of the earlier examples in this chapter, the reader will remember, involved the reaction to another commonplace experience, i.e., to object loss. Since every analyst has the opportunity to observe similar cases in his own practice, he should be able to convince himself from that best of teachers—his own experience—of the validity of the basis for a reconsideration of the relation between anxiety and conflict, the topic that will occupy the remainder of this chapter. The rationale for such a reconsideration may be familiar to some readers from two articles already published (Brenner, 1974b, 1975a). I shall not, however, assume that this is the case in what follows.

In his last major work on the subject Freud (1926) related psychic conflict to danger. He suggested that there is in the first years of life a developmentally determined sequence of danger situations: loss of object, loss of love, castration, and superego condemnation, i.e., guilt and punishment. Each typical danger situation, according to Freud, determines the content of the anxiety to which it gives rise. Thus psychic conflict may be initiated by fear of object loss, by fear of loss of love, by castration anxiety, by superego anxiety, or by any combination of the four. In psychoanalytic practice what one deals with are the consequences both in mental life and in behavior of the persistence of such conflicts, largely unconsciously, into later childhood and adulthood. Thus Freud postulated that the dynamics of psychic conflict in adult life as well as its origins in early childhood involve anxiety of one or more of the types just listed.

It has been frequently observed that the reformulation of the relation between anxiety and psychic conflict that Freud advanced in 1926 and that has been so briefly sketched in the paragraph above was an extremely fruitful one, that it permitted a much clearer and more accurate understanding of clinical phenomena, especially of analytic data, than had been possible previously, and that it is not too much to say that it inaugurated modern psychoanalytic technique. Certainly its fruitfulness is amply attested by the degree of its acceptance by psychoanalysts and psychoanalytically oriented psychiatrists during the years since it was introduced.

Yet the examples presented earlier in this chapter illustrate clearly that anxiety or, to be more exact, danger is not the only occasion for the initiation of psychic conflict, as analysts have, in general, believed to be the case since Freud's (1926) monograph appeared. How should Freud's theory, which has proved so useful for all these years, be amended or enlarged so that it will better fit the facts as we observe them in our analytic work?

The answer I have proposed is a fairly simple one. If, instead of relating conflict exclusively to anxiety we broaden our focus, as it were, by relating it to other intensely unpleasurable affects as well, I believe that we shall have no difficulty in accounting better for more of what we can observe as analysts. In doing so we shall be able to include and preserve Freud's essential contribution to the subject as one part of our new formulation.

Anxiety is a reaction to danger. Something bad, some calamity is about to happen. As we have seen, Freud suggested that there are four kinds of calamities or danger signals that are associated with psychic conflict. All four he subsumed under the general heading of a traumatic situation, which he defined as a situation of intense unpleasure. A traumatic situation, Freud said, can result from object loss (e.g., from maternal deprivation), from loss of love, from real or fantasied genital loss or injury, or from superego condemnation, these being the four typical calamities of early childhood. Whenever a traumatic situation, i.e., a situation of intense unpleasure, is anticipated, whatever its source may be, anxiety develops and defensive measures supervene. In other words, once a certain level of ego development has been reached (Brenner, 1953) the mere anticipation of the unpleasure of a traumatic situation suffices to produce unpleasure, specifically, the unpleasure of anxiety. Moreover, and it is this point that is essential to a more useful understanding of psychic conflict, according to Freud, what triggers defenses, what initiates conflicts, in such cases is the unpleasure which is a part of the affect we call anxiety (Brenner, 1974b). It is the operation of the pleasure principle that makes it necessary under certain circumstances, i.e. in situations of danger, for one to ward off or defend against drive derivatives. The following excerpts from "Inhibitions, Symptoms and Anxiety" (Freud, 1926) will serve to substantiate this statement.

> ...when [the ego] is opposed to an instinctual process in the id it has only to give a *'signal of unpleasure'* [= anxiety] in order to attain its object with the aid of that almost omnipotent institution, the pleasure principle [p. 92].

> ...as soon as the ego recognizes the danger of castration it gives the signal of anxiety and inhibits through the pleasure-unpleasure agency ... the impending cathectic process in the id [p. 125].

> ...anxiety sets symptom-formation [on p. 145 "symptom-formation" is emended to "defensive process"] going and is, indeed, a necessary prerequisite of it. For if the ego did not arouse the pleasure-unpleasure agency by generating anxiety, it would not obtain the power to arrest the process which is preparing in the id and which threatens danger [pp. 144-145].

As the clinical examples given earlier illustrate, what one observes in adult analytic patients and what one can reconstruct and observe, both directly and through analysis of childhood mental life, is that intense unpleasure associated with libidinal and aggressive wishes is not limited to danger situations, i.e., it is not present only as anxiety. It occurs also when one is convinced, whether consciously or unconsciously, whether by fact or in fantasy, that what is at other times only feared has actually happened—when one is sure that an important person is gone forever, that one is truly not loved or wanted, that one's genital organs are damaged or defective, or that one's misdeeds have been discovered and that one is being (has been) punished for them. Whether such a conviction is episodic, as it is in what Freud (1926) would have called a traumatic situation, or whether it is less intense, but long continued—what Kris (1956) and others have called "strain" traumas to distinguish them from acute "stress" traumas—it is in either case more than just a danger. It is something of the present and the past rather than of the future.

The essential point is that the unpleasure associated with such fantasies and experiences is quite as powerful a motive for defense and conflict as is the unpleasure of anxiety. For reasons presented more fully elsewhere (Brenner, 1974b) I have suggested that the term "depressive affect" be used to denote the broad range of affects that consist of unpleasure plus the conviction or awareness that a calamity—"something bad"—has happened, just as the term "anxiety" is currently used to denote the range of affects that consist of unpleasure plus the conviction or awareness that "something bad" is about to happen. We are then in a position to say that psychic conflict can and will be initiated by any sufficiently unpleasurable affect that is intimately connected with man's instinctual wishes, whether the affect be anxiety or depressive affect, i.e., whether the calamity be future, present, or past. When it is formulated in these terms and understood on this basis, one has no difficulty in applying a psychoanalytic theory of psychic conflict not only to the cases that conform satisfactorily to the familiar theory of the role of anxiety in psychic conflict (Freud, 1926) but to the cases that seem to be exceptions to it as well. It is clear that it is unpleasure, not merely anxiety, that initiates conflict.

It should be added that for a very young child there is often no clear distinction between the anticipation of a calamity and the conviction that a calamity has occurred. Just as, for a young child, wish and deed are equated, so are danger and reality in many instances. When this is so, it is as impossible as it is unnecessary to try to distinguish anxiety from depressive affect as the instigator of conflict. Whatever the affect, it is the fact of it being intensely unpleasurable that is significant both practically and in theory. Nonetheless there are many cases in which the distinction between the two affects is a real one, cases in which, as we have seen, it is the conviction that a calamity has occurred that has initiated — or has at least played an important part in initiating — a conflict whose consequences have caused a patient suffering and incapacity or worse.

As I have indicated elsewhere (Brenner, 1975a), when one relates conflict to intense unpleasure rather than exclusively to anxiety, certain corollaries follow that have practical significance. One of the most important of these has to do with patients in whom depressive affect plays a major role in their symptomatology. According to the theory proposed here, the proper approach in such cases is the same in principle as the approach to the analysis of anxiety when it plays a similarly important role in a patient's symptomatology: what is the ideational content of the affect, what are the instinctual and defensive components of the conflict and compromise formations of which it is a part, and what are its origins in early childhood and its vicissitudes in later life? In the case of anxiety "ideational content" means "dangers" or "danger situations." In the case of depressive affect "ideational content" means the calamity or calamities that a patient believes have befallen him already. Just as there is no such thing as "contentless" anxiety, or anxiety apart from danger, so there is no such thing as "contentless" depressive affect. The thoughts, memories, and fantasies that constitute the ideational content of either affect may be wholly or partially repressed, displaced, and otherwise defended against, as shown by several of the illustrative vignettes in this chapter as well as in the preceding ones, but they are always there to be inferred from the analytic material, sometimes readily and clearly, sometimes, to be sure, only with difficulty and uncertainty, but there nonetheless.

Clinical experience has shown that one of the most common sources of depressive affect and one of the most important as well is the superego (Beres, 1966). The ideational content of depressive affect often includes a conviction that one is alone, unloved, or castrated because one deserves to be so, a conviction that the calamity that has befallen one, whatever its nature, is a punishment for one's bad wishes or deeds. As we have seen earlier, for a child, his "bad deeds" include such things as the death, injury, or failure of his hated rivals. The point to be made here, however, is that just as fear of punishment gives rise to self-punitive trends in order to avoid superego anxiety, so may what is experienced as punishment itself give rise to the unpleasure of depressive affect and necessitate further defensive responses. Thus, for example, clinical experience tells us that a child who believes itself physically damaged, e.g., a little girl who believes herself to have been denied or deprived of her penis, often construes her deprivation as a punishment for her jealous, angry, and vengeful wishes.

The question naturally arises whether the defensive responses that are triggered by the unpleasure of depressive affect are the same as those triggered by the unpleasure of anxiety or whether there are significant differences. One's first thought would be that they must be the same, especially since we have already noted that the entire gamut of ego functions can, and at times does, serve the function of defending against derivatives of instinctual drives to avoid or minimize anxiety. From that point of view, indeed, there is no difference between defenses triggered by anxiety and those triggered by depressive affect. Any and all ego functions may be involved. There are differences, though, of another sort. For example, the entire range of psychic phenomena that are included under the headings of remorse, penance, propitiation, and even undoing are more apt to be used defensively in connection with the conviction that a calamity has occurred than in connection with the sense that one is impending. Exceptions will come readily to mind, but the statement seems likely to hold as a general rule. Moreover, depressive affect—the conviction that one has been abandoned, is unloved, is mutilated or defective, or is being punished—is very often associated with rage and other derivatives of aggression. As Reidy (1975) suggested, it is likely that the defensive aspect of such a reaction to an intensely unpleasurable calamity can be understood as identification with the aggressor, the aggressor being whoever, in the child's mind, is responsible for the calamity that has occurred.

Whatever the mixture may be of defense and gratification afforded by a reaction of rage in situations of intense unpleasure (Hartmann, Kris, and Loewenstein,

1949), one thing is certain. Rage gives rise to new problems, new anxieties that must be dealt with by defenses against the aggressive wishes that gave rise to them. In fact, the relationship between aggression and depressive affect in clinical practice is far more complex than has often been supposed. Each may intensify the other, as well as giving rise to fresh conflicts triggered by anxiety. And one may add that the validity and usefulness of broadening the theory of conflict as I have suggested, receive strong support from the fact that by doing so one is able to understand so much more clearly the complex interaction of depressive affect, anxiety, and aggression.

Additional support comes from a somewhat different direction, though not unrelated to the one just mentioned. When one broadens one's view of psychic conflict by relating it to unpleasure rather than to anxiety alone, one is no longer in the awkward position of being much better able to account theoretically for the oedipal conflicts of the male than of the female. Castration anxiety as a motive or occasion for conflict applies very well to the one, much less well to the other. It is true, as psychoanalytic authors have often observed, that many girls in the oedipal period have strong fears of genital injury that are quite analogous to the castration fears of boys of the same age. They are afraid of being torn or injured by what seem to them to be the huge penises of the fathers they desire sexually; they fear the loss of bowel contents that to them symbolize a penis they long to keep; they fear disfigurement or injury of one or another bodily part that symbolizes a penis, as they fear the loss of any other possession with the same symbolic value. Nevertheless, after one has taken all of this into account, it is clear that in most oedipal girls, if not in all, much more is involved than fear of loss and injury. There is in addition a great range of highly unpleasurable thoughts and feelings, which are intimately involved in the oedipal conflicts of females, that have little to do with anxiety and a great deal to do with what is usually referred to as penis envy. The term "penis envy" itself is a misleadingly restrictive one, as, e.g., Greenacre (1953) has pointed out. Much more is involved than envy alone in, for example, a girl's conviction that an irremediable and terrible catastrophe has befallen her—that she has been robbed of the penis she should have been born with, that she has lost it by masturbating, that she has forfeited it by her wish to replace her (penisless) mother, that she has been punished by its loss for her jealous and castrative wishes, and so on. The individual variations are endless even though the major themes are so few. This whole range of intensely unpleasurable reactions, intimately associated with instinctual wishes, comes under the heading of what we have called depressive affect, and as such its role in initiating conflict is readily understandable. In other words, with our new insight we can as easily account for oedipal conflicts in the female as in the male. In both, we can say, conflict is initiated by intensely unpleasurable affects that are a consequence of instinctual wishes. In both, defenses serve the purpose of avoiding or minimizing unpleasure. The main difference is that in girls depressive affect is likely to play the major role, in boys, anxiety. We must add to this statement not only that there are individual exceptions to this rule, but, in addition, that in every case, regardless of sex, some part is played by anxiety and some by depressive affect.

As one can see, there is already at hand evidence of substantial advantages from applying to clinical practice and to the understanding of psychoanalytic data the new theory of psychic conflict that has been outlined and discussed in this chapter. Time alone can tell how great those advantages may be. Not until sufficient experience has accumulated will it be possible to draw conclusions in a systematic and generally acceptable way. Until then one can say only that it seems to be a direction for psychoanalytic investigation that deserves exploration.

SUMMARY

1. Superego analysis presents a variety of technical problems. The most familiar problems are those associated with fear of punishment. In essence they are no different from the problems of defense analysis in general.

2. Defenses against fear of punishment (guilt, superego anxiety) present less familiar problems. Two illustrative vignettes are offered. In one, a patient's conscious guilt resulted from displacement as a defense against unconscious infantile guilt feelings. In the other, unconscious guilt gave rise to conscious ethical standards and a conscious moral judgment largely as a result of denial and reaction formation.

3. Still another aspect of superego analysis is related to phenomena of remorse and penance (reparation), along with defenses against them. A clinical example is offered that includes these as well as the phenomena of fear of punishment and defenses against fear of punishment (see previous paragraph) in order to illustrate some of the differences.

4. In many cases remorse and fear of punishment are related to the fulfillment and gratification of child-

hood instinctual wishes, i.e., not to fear of what will happen should those wishes be fulfilled, but rather to the fact that they have been. Such cases include those wrecked by success. Also included are persons whose whole lives are lived under the shadow of a need to do penance for the triumphant achievement of an infantile instinctual goal during childhood itself.

5. Finally, there are patients who feel the opposite of triumph. They feel already hurt and damaged by a calamity of childhood, whether that calamity be object loss, loss of love, castration, or some combination of the three. These patients include the "exceptions" of Freud (1916) and women in whose psychology penis envy plays a major role. Two vignettes are offered to illustrate the thesis that in instances of penis envy it is not anxiety that triggers conflict, but another closely related and equally unpleasurable affect, an affect related not to danger, as anxiety is, but to a calamity of the present or the past.

6. Consideration of these and related aspects of psychic conflict that are unrelated to superego functioning leads to a revision in the theory of conflict of the following sort. Instead of focusing exclusively on the role of anxiety in initiating conflict, a different formulation is suggested: psychic conflict is initiated by *any intensely unpleasurable affect related to the instinctual drives,* be it anxiety or what I suggest be called depressive affect. In the first case the "traumatic situation" is one of danger, in the second, a calamity that is happening or that has already occurred. In either case, it is *unpleasure* of whatever kind, not only anxiety, that serves as a trigger.

7. Some theoretical and practical advantages are discussed of thus revising our understanding of conflict by broadening it.

5

TRANSFERENCE

The reader will recall that Chapter 1 ended with some discussion of the importance that maintaining an analytic attitude can have in the management of transference. What was stressed there was that "acting naturally" toward an analytic patient is not the same as acting naturally in a different social situation or even in a different therapeutic situation. What would be natural behavior for a friend, an adviser, or a "good doctor" might be very unnatural and inappropriate behavior for an analyst. One cannot too often remind oneself that the relation between analyst and patient is a very special one. It is a therapeutic relation, to be sure, but it is unique among therapeutic relations. The very effectiveness of the therapy depends on the analyst's maintaining an analytic attitude, i.e., on his being nothing more and nothing less than an analyst, on his being guided consistently by the aim of helping his patient toward the goal of understanding the conflicts that give rise to his difficulties with the expectation that when he does understand them the difficulties they have caused will diminish substantially or disappear. For other forms of therapy a different relation between therapist and patient may be perfectly appropriate, even desirable, but for analysis nothing but an analytic attitude on the part of the therapist will do. The addition of a dash of encouragement, or a measure of scolding or admonition, however tactful and well intended, may seem to hasten the process. It can, at times, produce symptomatic improvement. But it is no substitute for analysis of *why* the patient wants encouragement, admonition, or any other nonanalytic behavior from 'iis analyst and in the long run it cannot fail to interfere to a greater or lesser degree with analytic progress and with the achievement of an optimal end result.

All of this has special relevance to any discussion of transference because it is analysis of the transference that is most affected when an analyst behaves other than analytically. Conversely, when in reality—in his actual behavior—an analyst limits himself to being his patient's analyst, the chances are best that his patient's transference wishes and fantasies will be perceived and understood by both patient and analyst; that they will, in a word, be analyzable.

The idea that any discussion of transference in relation to psychoanalytic technique should place emphasis on the analyzability of the transference is one that no experienced analyst will take exception to. Indeed many, if not all, might be expected to agree that analyzability of the transference should be the persistent and principal focus of any such discussion. Despite the general recognition of its importance, however, it is worthwhile to re-emphasize the fact, since it is the analyzability of the transference that is the key to the understanding of the true nature of the many problems concerning transference that have been so often discussed by successive generations of analysts. Insofar as they concern technique, *all* the problems that concern transference can be resolved into the single question of analyzability of transference wishes and fantasies.

Transference first came to Freud's attention as a manifestation of resistance to analysis (Freud, 1905). He soon realized, however, that it is by no means always merely resistance and by 1912 he had come to understand that transference develops inevitably in every successful analysis and, more than that, that it assists the analytic work in at least two ways. For one thing, it is the means or the opportunity for a patient to observe his unconscious, infantile wishes and conflicts *in statu nascendi* and to experience them in the present in an emotionally convincing way (Freud, 1912a, p. 108; 1914, p. 153). For another thing Freud believed at that time that at some point in every analysis an analyst must use his patient's positive transference as a lever to overcome his resistance to accepting the analyst's reconstruction of the origin of the patient's infantile conflicts themselves (Freud, 1917b, p. 445).

From these early discoveries there developed some conceptions that are still familiar and are still, on occasion, discussed and re-evaluated. One is the concept of transference neurosis and the question of its development. Another is the idea of a "benign positive transference." Still another is the concept of negative transference, and of the relationship between negative transference and resistance, along with the rule of thumb that transference should be analyzed only when it functions as resistance (see Brenner, 1969b). It was only after psychoanalytic theory had developed much farther in the direction of explaining the profound influence of infantile instinctual conflicts on object relations and on regressive alterations of such basic ego functions as perception, logic, action, and reality testing as a whole that it became possible to understand better the real meaning of the early concepts just mentioned, as well as of later ones, such as erotized transference, hostile transference, defense transference, acting out of the transference, therapeutic (or working) alliance, and even the recommendation, so strenuously urged by Strachey (1934) and others, that only a transference interpretation can be truly "mutative" in its effect on a patient. Each of these concepts and recommendations contains something of value since each, after all, was based on a perceptive observation of important clinical, analytic data, and the present state of psychoanalytic theory permits one to extract from each what is valuable and to include it in a more general explanatory conceptual framework.

As Freud realized at the start and as he indicated by the word he used—transference (*Übertragung* in German)—the essence of the whole matter is that in analysis every patient's thoughts, wishes, feelings, and fantasies about his analyst recapitulate unconscious thoughts, feelings, wishes, and fantasies that originated in the instinctual life of childhood. Infantile wishes, etc., that were originally concerned with the important persons of childhood and that are still concerned with those persons unconsciously, become transferred—whence the term—to the person of the analyst. The major conflicts—wishes, fears, defenses, guilt feeling, and compromise formations

—of early childhood reappear, as it were, in the patient's relationship with his analyst, i.e., in the analytic situation. What was not realized, nor even realizable when transference was first recognized, is that what has just been described happens in *every* adult relationship, not just in the relationship between patient and analyst. The unconscious instinctual derivatives, and the associated anxiety, depressive affect, defenses, and guilt—in a word, the unconscious conflicts originating in childhood—appear in every adult object relationship and determine the very nature of each one. It is not true that this happens more regularly in the psychoanalytic situation than elsewhere. It happens every time. It's not even true that the importance of psychic conflicts of childhood origin is greater in the relation between patient and analyst than it is in other relationships. As Freud (1915) remarked, there is no fundamental psychological difference between transference love and "ordinary" love. The dynamics— the influence of infantile, conflictual factors—are the same in both. What distinguish an analytic relationship from any other are not the *dynamics* of the transference but its *place* in the relationship, i.e., the analyst's attitude toward the transference and the use he makes of it. It is the analytic attitude that is the hallmark of analysis, not the phenomena subsumed under the heading of transference. The latter are ubiquitous. It is the former that is unique.

In principle, therefore, it is not difficult to say how one deals with the transference in psychoanalysis. One deals with it just as one does with any other aspect of a patient's mental activity and behavior. One forms conjectures about the nature of the psychic conflicts that cause it and about their origins in early childhood and one communicates one's conjectures to the patient in the form of interpretations at the proper time. The principle is easy—it is to analyze. It is the application of the principle in practice that is often difficult or impossible, not the principle itself. Let us see, then, what can be said about its application that may be helpful.

First of all it is apparent from the preceding discussion that transference is *always* present. A patient's psychic conflicts, originating as they do from the instinctual wishes of childhood, will always enter into his relationship with his analyst for the same reasons that they will always enter into his relationship with every person in his adult life. Transference, as we have said already, is not something that happens only sometimes or only with some patients. It happens always with every patient. It is true that some patients, because of the nature of their conflicts, will appear to have no thoughts or feelings of a personal nature about their analyst, but the appearance is always deceptive. A patient may deny, ignore, or otherwise defend himself against such thoughts and feelings. He may react so negatively, so suspiciously, or with such a need to withdraw from the analyst that analysis becomes impossible. But that does not mean that there is no transference. On the contrary, the indifference, the lack of conscious emotion, the absence of conscious personal interest, the suspiciousness, the antagonism, the withdrawal *are* the manifestations of transference. Such a transference reaction may be an insuperable resistance, but it results from the psychic conflicts of infantile origin of the particular patient in whom it appears just as much as does an analyzable transference reaction in another patient. More than that, it gives some hint as to the nature of the conflicts that have produced it, even when it is impossible to test one's conjecture about its nature by the usual analytic means. In a word, then, whatever a patient's reaction to his analyst may be, wishes, fears, and defenses originating in childhood have an important part in it.

When analysis can go forward, in fact, one is able to observe that it makes no difference whether a patient is conspicuously a "good" patient or whether he is as conspicuously "bad" from the very first day of analysis on. In any case his psychic conflicts influence his attitude and behavior toward his analyst, whether for better or for worse, as the following vignettes illustrate.

A 29-year-old married woman seemed from the first like an ideal analytic patient. She came to her sessions eagerly, spoke freely with only occasional pauses, had ample affective display, could relate present problems to childhood experiences, reported dreams and associated to them—all in a most gratifying way. As analysis proceeded it soon became apparent that she was terrified of her (largely unconscious) murderous and suicidal wishes and that her chief fear was of being abandoned as she had been repeatedly from as far back as she could remember—certainly before the age of three. Her last childhood banishment had been to boarding school in the eighth and ninth grades. Thereafter she had been able to live at home until she went off to college by her own choice three years later. Through the ninth grade the patient had been a troublesome, rebellious girl. She was constantly getting into scrapes both at home and in school and she fought openly with her mother and with her teachers. She was never seriously delinquent—just a naughty, aggressive girl. Beginning in the tenth grade, however, her relationship with her mother changed remarkably. She became her good friend and companion. Every day after school she sat with her mother for half an hour or an hour and chatted with her about school, about friends, about plans, events of the moment — about anything that was on her mind. And she stayed at home for three whole years. She became a companionable daughter instead of a troublesome, rebellious one. She warded off any direct expression of her aggression out of fear of being sent away, and she remained her mother's friend and companion thereafter. For this patient, then, intimate conversation on a daily basis had become both a way of gratifying her wish for her mother's love and attention and an important defense against aggressive derivatives that brought with them the danger of object loss and loss of love. It was, if not a symptom, at least a compromise formation that resembled a symptom in every important respect, and that dated back to the patient's sixteenth year. And, as might be expected, it appeared in the analysis as part of the transference. She talked to me each day, as she had done with her mother years before, in order to win my love and approval as well as to ward off the aggressive wishes she unconsciously feared would result in her losing me forever by one of us dying, by my banishing her, or by her running away. It was only after this aspect of her transference had been understood and interpreted that this previously "good" analytic patient became conscious of her desire to forget or conceal the horrifying destructive fantasies that occupied her attention off and on during the day — fantasies that until then she hadn't "noticed" enough to remember.

A second patient showed just the opposite sort of behavior in analysis. He was a "bad" patient right from the start, so much so that for years it seemed unlikely that he would ever be capable of any real analytic progress. It was imperative for him that he assure himself constantly that he was in complete control—that he was the boss, not I—that he was not an underling, a victim, or a woman. Such a transference reaction is far from rare. What made it so unusually intense in this patient as to be nearly unmanageable even after it was fairly well understood was the fact that the patient had previously been in treatment with a therapist who had "psychoanalyzed" him with results that were disastrous for the patient. At the time treatment ended, and for many months previously, the two were locked in a sadomasochistic relationship that neither understood and that was impossible for them to resolve. What the patient experienced was that he was scolded, belittled, and ridiculed for his symptoms at the same time that he felt more and more hopelessly incapacitated and in desperate need of his therapist's advice and encouragement. A more severe negative therapeutic reaction would be hard to imagine in the setting of an office practice, i.e., outside a mental hospital. As a result, after he entered treatment with me this patient's transference required for its resolution an unusual length of time as well as a degree both of toleration of "bad" behavior, i.e., open defiance and stubbornness, and of caution in making interpretations for the first many months of treatment, that is also unusual in adult analysis. The point that is important for our purpose, however, is that this patient's "bad" behavior, no less that the first patient's "good" behavior was a manifestation of transference. Both patients were eager for treatment and willing to cooperate before treatment began, but neither could help acting as he or she did once treatment had started until the reasons for the behavior of each, i.e., its conflict-laden determinants, could be analyzed.

In both these patients there was an unusual degree of urgency about their transference reactions quite early in their analyses. The transference had to be understood and interpreted early because from the start of analysis it occupied the center of the stage in each patient's analytic material. The most striking thing about the first patient was how fluently she talked without ever revealing anything that really troubled or upset her, anything she felt was a real problem to her. Once this became apparent, it became equally apparent that it was necessary to understand why it was so, i.e., to analyze it. When it was analyzed, as has been said above, it turned out that it was a consequence or manifestation of transference—that it was a repetition of what she had done with her mother from the age of fifteen onward. The most striking thing about the second patient from the very beginning was his behavior, which was at once controlling, stubborn, and defiant. It too demanded analytic attention, therefore, and it too turned out to be part of the transference.

In other patients there is no such urgency about analyzing the transference at the very beginning of treatment. This does not mean that transference is absent or even unimportant in those patients. It means only that for the moment other things take analytic precedence. In every case the time will come when the transference becomes more prominent and must be analyzed.

Freud (1914) made the point, already referred to, that it is only through analysis of the transference that a patient is fully convinced of the intensity of the conflicts underlying his symptoms and of the ways in which those conflicts distort his perception of reality, i.e., of his analyst's attitude and behavior toward him, as well as of the degree to which they do so. There is no doubt that this is often the case, though it seems unlikely that it is either correct or useful to take the extreme position that Strachey (1934) advocated. He insisted that, in psychoanalysis, real insight and real psychic change can be produced only by an interpretation of one or another aspect of the transference.

On the basis of my own experience as analyst and teacher I am tempted to add to Freud's observation what one might call its converse. It has seemed to me that, for many analysts, a full appreciation of the intensity of psychic conflicts and of their ability to influence, to distort, and even to overturn altogether such basically important ego functions as logical thought, perception, memory, and reality testing, comes only from analysis of the transference manifestations of their patients. The *sine qua non* for such an understanding is one's personal analysis, but to appreciate to their full extent the power that psychic conflicts of infantile origin exert on virtually every aspect of mental functioning one must see them in action in one patient after another, and for that there is no better opportunity than the one offered by observation and analysis of the transference in psychoanalytic practice. Its educative potential is second to none.

To return to the subject of "good" and "bad" patients, the two vignettes just offered can also be used to support and illustrate a proposition that is of fundamental importance for psychoanalytic technique, the proposition that a patient's ability to cooperate in analysis, his ability to associate freely in a meaningful way, depends primarily on the conscious and unconscious anxiety, guilt, and depressive affect that his doing so cause him.

To put the matter in different language, one can say that resistance in general is a function of unpleasure, i.e., of anxiety, guilt, and depressive affect, and that resistance due to transference wishes and conflict is no exception. Every difficulty posed for analysis by the relationship between analyst and patient comes down to this fundamental factor, whatever the name may be that has been coined for it. Transference resistance in an analytic patient is necessarily a consequence of the patient's conflict due to unpleasure associated with sexual and aggressive wishes toward his analyst, conflicts that mirror and repeat in the analytic situation ones that originated in the patient's childhood and that impelled him to seek analysis in the first place.

One of the many applications of this proposition is to the understanding of what is called the therapeutic or working alliance (Zetzel, 1956, 1966; Greenson, 1967, pp. 45-48; Sandler et al., 1970). These terms are useful at times in referring to certain consequences of transference resistance, such as a patient's willingness or ability to speak freely and to agree with his analyst's interpretations. They have the disadvantage, however, of deflecting attention from the factors that are of principal importance in producing the consequences just mentioned and others like them. The ability of any patient to cooperate productively in analysis is directly dependent on unpleasure and conflict, as the two vignettes above illustrate. A "good" analytic patient is expected to come to his analyst's office regularly at the appointed time, to lie on a couch, and to speak freely about whatever comes to his mind, whether it be current, everyday activities, childhood menories, or thoughts about his analyst; whether it be sexual matters, dreams, fantasies, or bodily sensations;

whether it be joy, sorrow, anger, longing, or disappointment. He is, moreover, expected to associate to whatever he is asked to associate to—to dreams, to slips, to transient sensations, to symptoms, for example—and to listen to whatever intervention or interpretation his analyst makes. All of this he is expected to take seriously, i.e., not to dismiss it, to shrug it off, or to pay no attention to it. If any or all of these things would bring with it too much unpleasure, the patient will not do it. Sometimes he's aware that there's something he's avoiding or not doing, sometimes he isn't. Rarely is he conscious of his motives, of *why* he's behaving as he is. When, as in the vignettes above, the intensity of the unpleasure associated with "good" analytic behavior is very great, the deviation from the desired ideal is gross and long-lasting. But in every case there are bound to be times when a patient fails to do something in his analysis that he does at other times as a matter of course, since he believes it to be in his own best interest to do it. These times may be short or long. They may last a few minutes, an hour, a week, or many months. Whenever they are more than very mild and very brief they may require analysis of their conflictual determinants, like any other intercurrent symptom. What is less desirable is to attempt to induce a patient to control any such "bad" analytic behavior by encouragement, by suasion, by disapproval, or by scolding, however friendly and well-intentioned such attempts may be. Any such non-analytic behavior by the analyst will only complicate the transference. If there is very much of such behavior, it may complicate the transference to such a degree that it becomes unanalyzable. It is just this possibility that is the chief danger of the concept of a therapeutic or working alliance between patient and analyst. The concept, that is, may lead to the mistaken notion that such an alliance is something special, something that it is an analyst's responsibility to foster and a patient's to maintain. Just the opposite is the case. It is not something special or different. Any deviation from "good" analytic behavior by a patient is, like any other symptom, a consequence of psychic conflict, an indication that conflict is active, and a hint at least as to what the conflict is. Whenever a patient's behavior qua patient deviates from the analytic ideal sufficiently for it to seem useful to bring it to his attention, it should be done in an analytic way. A patient's desire to avoid a particular topic, for one example, or a particular time of his life, for another, or to fail to report certain thoughts, for a third, are things to bring to his attention for him to think and talk about—in a word, to analyze—not for him to control, to suppress, or to overcome because they are undesirable defections from his alliance with his analyst. To speak epigrammatically, it is good analytic technique to facilitate the expression of any wish or need that a patient has to be a "bad" analytic ally.

It is important to add that the advice that an analyst should deal with transference resistances of this sort by analyzing them does not imply that he will find doing so always easy, or even possible. One reason why analysis is such a long, slow, arduous task is that it is no easy matter for anyone to become aware of wishes and memories that have all his life been too unpleasurable to acknowledge. Intensity of conflict and degree of unpleasure, if not synonymous, are at least closely related phenomena. Both profoundly influence the ease or difficulty of analysis. The more intense the underlying conflict, the more unpleasure involved with it, the greater will be a patient's resistance to analysis, whatever the analytic material may be.

The same general considerations that we have just made use of in our discussion of the phenomena referred to by the terms therapeutic and working alliance can be applied as well to other problems that arise in the course of analysis as vicissitudes of the transference. Take, for example, transference acting out (Freud, 1914). How would one understand it today and how would one deal with it in analysis?[1]

First of all, one should remember that behavior motivated by transference wishes is a frequent occurrence in every analysis. A patient's report of his actions outside the analytic hour and his associations to them are an important source of information about the transference as well as an important confirmation of conjectures concerning it in every analysis. They are often just as useful in this respect as are fantasies, dreams, symptoms, etc. It is an analytic commonplace that a patient's quarrel with his employer, his teacher, or some other person in his everyday life may be the result of an unconscious wish to quarrel with his analyst. Similarly, an unconscious reluctance to pay his analyst, motivated by infantile sexual wishes, may lead a patient to arrange his finances unconsciously in such a way as to make it necessary for him to pay his analyst a few days later than usual. In still another patient transference wishes may give rise to flirtatiousness outside the analysis, to a new love affair, or to

[1] Acting out was the principal topic of discussion at the 1967 Congress of the International Psycho-Analytical Association. See A. Freud (1968), Grinberg (1968), Schwarz (1968), Moore (1968), Rouart (1968), Mitscherlich-Nielsen (1968), Garbarino (1968), Rangell (1968), Lebovici (1968), Vanggaard (1968), Greenacre (1968), Demaria (1968), Atkins (1968), and Report (1968); see also Brenner (1969b).

temporary frigidity or asceticism. Examples like these are so common in every analyst's practice that no illustrations are necessary. Since actions outside the analytic setting are so often motivated by transference wishes and conflicts as to be commonplace analytic material, it is clear that the only reason for calling some of them by a special name—acting out—is that some of them are refractory to analysis and may even interfere with its progress to a significant degree. The idea seems to be that if they're analyzable, they're just manifestations of the transference that need no special name; if they're not analyzable, they're acting out.

One can see, therefore, that in the light of our current understanding of the importance of psychic conflict in the motivation of action in general, it is at best ambiguous and at worst misleading to give a special name to some of a patient's behavior during analysis simply because it is more difficult to analyze than is other behavior. To do so runs the risk of conveying the idea that the behavior called acting out is dynamically different from other behavior of analytic patients and even that acting out behavior is so different dynamically that it is best treated by forbidding it or by advising against it, rather than by trying to analyze it in the usual way. The facts are precisely the opposite. There is no difference dynamically between actions that are readily analyzable, and hence useful in analysis, and those less readily analyzable, and hence an obstacle to analytic work, just as there is no difference dynamically between a dream that is analyzable when reported and one that is understood only months or years later. What determines the use that can be made of any such material at a particular time in analysis is, as we have said, the intensity of the conflict of which it is a product. The more intense the conflict, the greater the potential unpleasure that has triggered it, the greater the resistance on a patient's part to analysis of it and its results. Sometimes analysis is impossible, sometimes it can proceed only very slowly over a period of many years, sometimes it can be done more quickly, but whatever the outcome, the procedure and the principles on which the procedure depends remain the same. Persuasion and suggestion are not analysis. They may produce welcome symptomatic improvement, but they cannot serve the purposes of analysis as we understand analysis today. The actions of an analytic patient are one source of analytic material and are to be analyzed like any other when it is useful and possible to do so.

Two more points before we leave the subject of acting out. First, it is a little misleading to refer to an element or a manifestation of transference as analyzable or not. No analytic material is ever likely to be completely analyzed. One never expects to understand everything about the dynamics and origins of any patient's psychic conflicts. Even at the end of a long and successful analysis there are questions still unanswered. It is more precise, therefore, not to refer to transference as analyzable or unanalyzable, but rather as understandable and manageable analytically or as unmanageable analytically, where the word "analytically" is understood to mean "by analytic means in an analytic situation." For short, one will do better to call transference analytically manageable or unmanageable rather than analyzable or unanalyzable. Second, a common reason for transference behavior that is analytically unmanageable is undue delay in interpreting to a patient his transference wishes and conflicts, whether the delay be due to a failure on the analyst's part to understand them or whether it be for some other reason. Please note the word "undue." Timing of interpretations is not an exact science. There is not just a single right moment for presenting an interpretation to a patient. Correct timing means only not long before a patient is ready nor very long after he was first ready. If an analyst is confronted by transference manifestations that are analytically unmanageable, e.g., so-called acting out, one of the questions he should ask himself is whether he has failed to interpret an important aspect of the transference to his patient in good time (Fenichel, 1945). It should be added that acting out on this basis is but one variety of the consequences of delaying too long in interpreting a patient's transference. Freud (1905) first recognized the importance of perceiving, understanding, and interpreting manifestations of transference when his failure to do so resulted in one of his patients leaving treatment abruptly. In general, undue delay in interpreting a patient's transference leads to more or less severe resistance on his part to the analysis and in some cases this resistance takes the form of action of the sort that is called acting out.

In general it may be said, then, that whether a transference in analysis is manageable by purely analytic means will depend very much on an analyst's ability to maintain an analytic attitude consistently (see Chapter 1). The better an analyst is able to do this, the more likely he is to succeed in making analytic use of the transference, i.e., of the largely unconscious conflict-laden wishes of his patient that stem from childhood and that involve his analyst in the therapeutic situation. As the examples at the end of Chapter 1 indicate, it is necessary to bear this in mind when one is dealing with what are so often referred to as reality factors in the analytic relationship. One must not forget that transference wishes and conflicts are just as real a part of a patient's mental life as is anything else that currently concerns him. More than that, one must bear in mind that, in addition to being a very real part of every patient's mental life, transference wishes and conflicts are often the most important determinants of a patient's conscious thoughts, emotions, and actions, however little he may be conscious that this is the case. The proper division is not between transference and reality. The proper division is between what is a truly important factor in determining a patient's thoughts, his emotions, and his actions, and what is in fact less important, or even unimportant, however important it may seem on the surface to be, especially to the patient himself.

Thus, for example, the "real personality" of an analyst is important only as a patient perceives it and reacts to it. It is a stimulus to a patient's mental activity like any other. The patient's reaction to it must be analyzed before one can tell what is real to him. This is not to say that an analyst's appearance, manner, way of speaking, and surroundings are unimportant. They are very important, but their effect will never be the same on any two patients and is often very different on the same patient at different times in his analysis. It is reasonable to expect, to be sure, if an analyst is very unconventional in one way or another, and still more if he is unusually inconsiderate, roughly disapproving, or ingratiatingly seductive, that any or all of those characteristics of behavior and attitude will interfere more or less seriously with the analytic progress of many of his patients. Nevertheless, even in such an extreme and obviously undesirable case the nature of the interference will be different for every patient and only if it can be analyzed can one hope to know what it actually is.

Suppose an analyst were to fall asleep during a session, or to forget an appointment with a patient. Should he apologize, explain and discuss the reasons for his action with his patient? Many analysts would say he should (see, e.g., Greenson, 1974), and their arguments for doing so are persuasive. Yet I believe the better course to follow is the usual one of encouraging a patient to express *his* thoughts and feelings about what has happened. Only in that way can one learn whether a patient has taken his analyst's mistake as a slight that has offended and angered him, or as a sign of weakness that allows him to feel superior and even triumphant, or as a welcome excuse for anger, etc. A conscientious analyst will naturally regret such a mistake, he will certainly try, through self-analysis, to discover his unconscious reasons for having acted as he did, but he will be well advised to maintain an analytic attitude even to such an event and not to assume what it must mean to his patient without hearing what his patient has to say. It is presumptuous to act the analyst, unbidden, in a social or family situation. It is a technical lapse to be other than an analyst in one's relation with an analytic patient. However well it is rationalized, the temptation to be anything but an analyst when one is in an analytic situation should be resisted. In every instance what one says or does should be determined by one's attitude of concern to learn as much as possible of the nature and origins of each patient's conflicts in order to help him do the same.

If one keeps this general principle always in mind, one has little difficulty with such matters as whether to interpret transference *only* when it is a resistance to progress, whether every interpretation must be a transference interpretation, how to deal with hostile or negative transference, how to deal with an "erotic" transference, etc. In every case the answer will depend on one's understanding of the nature and origins of that particular patient's conflicts and of their role in his current thoughts and behavior. Transference should be neither ignored nor focused on to the exclusion of all else; it should be neither excluded from the analytic work nor dragged in by the heels. As a practical matter, transference bulks much larger in analytic work than the uninitiated imagine can be the case. Its influence often is greater even than one assumed it to be at the beginning of one's analytic career, despite one's reading and one's own personal experience in analysis. Nevertheless it remains but one factor among many in any analytic situation. An analyst has always the task of deciding as best he can from the available evidence which factors are the most important at a particular time in the analysis. His analytic course of action must depend on that decision. If an analyst's conjecture (understanding) is that transference factors are of principal importance, it is on them that his interpretations to his patient will focus. If his conjecture, be it conscious or unconscious, intuitive or reasoned, is that something other than the transference is most important at the moment, he will interpret whatever the "something other" may be.

We may profitably conclude this chapter with some discussion of the subject of countertransference. As the reader may have noticed, the suppositious example given above, in which an analyst fell asleep, is an example of countertransference, since for an analyst to fall asleep

during an analytic hour, some powerful motive must
ordinarily be supposed to be at work in his mind—a
motive that is wholly or partly unconscious.

From what has been said earlier in the chapter about
the nature of transference and especially about its relationship to object relations in general it should be clear
that an analyst's thoughts and feelings about his patients
have unconscious infantile components just as theirs do
about him. This is something, as we have said, that holds
true for every object relationship. In the case of the transference, the question is not whether such components
exist, but whether they can be dealt with by the usual
analytic means. In the case of the countertransference
similar considerations hold good, as will appear in the
following discussion.

An analyst's desire to understand his patient's unconscious conflicts must itself have unconscious, infantile
roots—roots he learns about in his own analysis. So must
his reaction to whatever his patient's conflicts may be,
and they vary from patient to patient, as all analysts
know. Some patients' conflicts will be closer to an analyst's own—to the wishes, the fears, the joys, and the
disasters of his own childhood—while others will be more
distant from those events and memories. If, as a result of
his own analysis, an analyst is not too disturbed by being
reminded of his own conflicts, he will be able to understand and interpret those of his patients, even if they
come close to his own, once he has acquired the necessary
knowledge of analytic technique and has some degree of
experience in applying it. In other words, his countertransference will not interfere unduly with his ability to
function as an analyst. It will not impede the progress of
his patient's analysis.

This is not to say, however, that countertransference does not exist in a well-analyzed analyst. Whatever work one does as an adult, whatever satisfactions one finds in a chosen profession, whatever relationships one establishes with persons one meets and deals with, whether in a professional capacity or in any other, all are significantly motivated and determined by psychic conflicts that originated in connection with childhood instinctual wishes. One cannot, therefore, distinguish sharply between countertransference that deserves to be called normal and that which deserves to be called pathological (see Freud, 1910; Heimann, 1950; Little, 1951; Money-Kyrle, 1956; Reich, 1951). Just as in the case of neurotic symptoms, the differences are a matter of degree: the degree of interference with or inhibition of function—in this case, the ability to analyze—the degree of associated unpleasure, fatigue or anhedonia, the guilt, the penance, the remorse, etc. When they are applied to the phenomenon of countertransference, "normal" and "pathological" are meaningful words only if they designate, respectively, derivatives of psychic conflict that are not seriously disadvantageous to analysis or are even helpful and advantageous to it, and derivatives of psychic conflict that are seriously or, at the very least, are significantly disadvantageous to analysis.

SUMMARY

1. Unconscious instinctual conflicts of infantile origin determine the nature of every adult relationship. In other words, transference factors are universal and ubiquitous. They are not limited to the analytic situation, nor even dynamically more important there than elsewhere.

2. It is an analyst's attitude toward the transference and the use he makes of it that are the hallmarks of analysis, not the presence of the transference and its dynamic importance. In analysis the transference is to be analyzed in the usual analytic way—it is to be understood and interpreted.

3. Transference is equally characteristic of "good" analytic patients and of "bad" ones. There is no such thing as a patient who has "no transference," or in whom transference "fails to develop."

4. It is from the analysis of the transference reactions of his patients that an analyst gains a full appreciation of the intensity of psychic conflicts in the mind of man and of their ability to influence, to distort, and even to overturn altogether such basically important ego functions as logical thought, perception, memory, and reality testing.

5. Transference resistance stems from the unpleasure associated with the instinctual wishes of a patient concerning his analyst.

6. The "working" or "therapeutic" alliance is one of the many aspects of the transference. Its vicissitudes in the course of an analysis are best dealt with by analyzing them rather than in nonanalytic ways.

7. Actions that are largely motivated by the transference appear in every analysis. Those that have been called acting out are the ones that are not readily analyzable, especially if they constitute a serious obstacle (resistance) to the treatment. Whatever their importance as a resistance, transference-motivated actions are best dealt with by the usual analytic methods of conjecture and interpretation.

8. Manifestations of transference, whatever their nature, may or may not be analyzable. "Analyzable" and "unanalyzable" transference mean, respectively, transfer-

ence manifestations that are or are not understandable and manageable by analytic means in an analytic situation.

9. The distinction between "reality factors" and "transference factors" in an analytic situation is a specious one. Transference is just as real as are current environmental influences, i.e., what is meant by "external reality," and both are always present and active in a patient's mind. The important distinction for technical purposes in analysis is between situations in which transference factors play a sufficiently large role to warrant interpretation and those in which they do not.

10. Like transference, countertransference is ubiquitous, since derivatives of infantile instinctual conflicts play a significant part in every adult object relationship and in every vocational activity of adult life.

11. Like transference, countertransference may assist analysis or may hinder it, depending on the circumstances.

12. The most useful general principle to apply to whatever technical problems may arise either from transference or from countertransference is to maintain an analytic attitude, i.e., to attempt to understand the nature and origins of the psychic conflicts that underlie a patient's thoughts, feelings, and behavior.

6

ANALYSIS OF DREAMS, SYMPTOMS, FANTASIES, AND SIMILAR PHENOMENA

There was a time when psychoanalysis was described, almost defined, as the psychotherapy that used dream analysis. Freud (1905), for example, wrote a paper to illustrate the value that dream analysis can have in analytic treatment. Sachs (personal communication, 1942) made a practice of continuing the analysis of a dream from one session to the next. If he felt a dream had not been sufficiently well understood, he would conclude an hour by saying so to his patient and would add, "We'll have to spend more time on it tomorrow." Balint (1961) had each candidate who was in analysis with him analyze one of his own dreams as completely as possible before he terminated his analysis. Such a thorough dream analysis might take as long as a week, he said. The exercise was intended to give each candidate a real understanding of how much a dream can tell about a patient — in this case, the candidate himself — if it can only be fully analyzed.

Thus dream analysis has long had a special position in psychoanalytic treatment. Many analysts still consider it to be the surest and fastest route to the discovery of the nature and origin of a patient's psychic conflicts, as Freud (1900, p. 608) said it was when he first wrote on the subject. One consequence of its special position is that dream analysis has been taught and its place in analytic technique has been emphasized at the expense of attention to such other mental phenomena as daydreams, slips, metaphors, jokes, reactions to books, films, or plays, and even neurotic symptoms. Every psychoanalytic institute with whose curriculum I am familiar has at least one course or seminar on dream analysis. Many have two or three. I know of none with a course on symptom analysis. All institutes have courses on the dynamics and genesis of symptoms, to be sure, but not, to my knowledge, on symptom analysis. It is interesting in this connection to observe that Lewin (1952) thought it worthwhile to write a paper to demonstrate that phobic symptoms can indeed by analyzed just as dreams can be. Considering the fact that what patients come to analysis for is relief of symptoms of one sort or another, it is hard to understand why symptom analysis should be so neglected in psychoanalytic curricula. As for daydreams, etc., they are hardly mentioned in courses on technique. The psychology of such phenomena may be discussed in one or another seminar, but not their place in clinical analytic work.

No analyst will doubt the usefulness of dream analysis in psychoanalytic treatment. But precisely because its value is universally accepted and its technique and application so well understood, it is less necessary to re-emphasize them here. The greater emphasis in this chapter on the analysis of other features of mental life must be understood as an attempt to redress the imbalance caused by their relative neglect elsewhere in the psychoanalytic literature. It is not meant to suggest that dreams are even relatively less important as objects of analysis than other phenomena to which more space will be given here than is usually the case.

We shall begin with some remarks on dream analysis in clinical practice that are, perhaps, an addition to what is well known on the subject and has been said many times.

First of all it may be noted that for a long time the chief importance of dream analysis lay in the opportunities it afforded for discovering a patient's pathogenic instinctual wishes and the repressed memories associated with them. Analysts used dream analysis as a principal means of access to repressed wishes of the system Ucs. and as a basis for reconstructing the pathologically significant events of childhood. After the introduction of the structural theory (Freud, 1923a) and the reappraisal of the role of anxiety in psychic conflict (Freud, 1926), the scope of dream analysis and interpretation was correspondingly enlarged. The focus of attention was no longer exclusively on childhood instinctual wishes. It was altered so as to include in the field all the other elements of conflict: anxiety, guilt, defense, and such superego elements as self-punishment and penance. For most analysts this substantial alteration in practice did not entail any corresponding revision of theory. Analysts in general seemed content, as Lewin (1952) expressed himself, to use the newer structural theory when analyzing neurotic symptoms and character traits while retaining the topographic theory when dealing with dreams. Arlow and I (1964) demonstrated some of the practical disadvantages and logical inconsistencies that result from such a theoretical dichotomy in one's approach to dreams and dream analysis. In the same monograph we elaborated a revised theory of dream psychology, based on an earlier exposition (Brenner, 1955), the essence of which is that a dream is a compromise formation like any other compromise among id, ego, and superego. Its special psychological features are not best explained by the theory originally proposed to explain them (Freud, 1900), i.e., by postulating that dream formation begins in the system Ucs. according to the primary process and that it is only subsequently that it is subjected to the secondary process by the system Pcs., which both acts as a censor and imposes on the dream elements a kind of logical or editorial revision. On the contrary, a dream is from the very start a compromise among the three systems of the mind, like any waking thought, fantasy, or action. The special psychological features that characterize dreams are readily explained by assuming a degree of regression and suspension of ego functions during sleep. In particular, the sense of reality that is so characteristic of most dreams results from the suspension of reality testing during sleep. In contrast with adult, waking like, during sleep fancy is accepted as fact, just as it so often is during childhood.

What are the advantages of revising the psychoanalytic theory of the psychology of dreaming in this way? For one thing, what were exceptions to the old theory are consonant with its revision. This is true of punishment dreams, for example, as well as for dreams in which a sense of reality is *not* maintained throughout the dream, as when a dreamer thinks to himself, "It's only a dream."

For another thing, it makes explicit a feature of dreams in general that might otherwise escape attention. Unintelligibility in dreams is always a consequence of defense. It doesn't result from the fact that dream thoughts have been "translated into the primary process," as though that were analogous to translation into an unfamiliar foreign language. Dreams may well be unintelligible to anyone other than the dreamer for a variety of reasons, but when the dreamer himself does not know what the wishes are that he imagines fulfilled in his dream it is invariably because of a need to avoid or minimize the unpleasure due to anxiety, guilt, or depressive affect that his wishes would arouse were they not disguised, distorted, and otherwise defended against. Finally, it seems to me that perhaps the chief value of the revision suggested by Arlow and myself is that it places dreams in a proper perspective among the great variety of mental phenomena. They are no longer to be thought of as a sort of exception, as phenomena *suorum generorum,* but rather as subject to the same general laws as are other mental phenomena and understandable in the same conceptual framework. In this respect then our revision conforms to Freud's original aim, that of relating dream psychology to the psychology of neurotic symptom formation, the psychology of such everyday phenomena as slips and errors, and eventually to the psychology of jokes as well.

If we turn now from such broad and general considerations to something much more limited, there is one feature of dream analysis that is worth spending some time on. What is usually referred to as the text of a dream, or its manifest content, is never the dream itself. It is only what the dreamer—in our context, the patient—

tells us. If one is willing to be precise about it, one will admit that in fact one can never know the manifest content of another person's dream. One can only try to reconstruct it from the dreamer's account of it. One's first reaction to this admission may be some sense of disappointment or even of disillusionment, but a moment's reflection will suffice to dispel it. After all, what is important in analysis is not a "dream," it is what the dream means—what it can tell us about the dreamer. It is, in fact, a great advantage that the report of any dream is actually a statement of the dreamer's first, spontaneous associations to it. The words he uses, insofar as they are not repetitions of words that appeared in the dream itself, his tone of voice, his affect as he tells of his dream—in a word, the whole of the "manifest content"—are all doubly valuable precisely because they are not just his memory of a conscious experience during sleep, they are his associations to it as well. Keeping this fact in mind is helpful because otherwise one may be tempted to try to get as clear and full a description of a dream as possible from a patient, as though that's what one should do before asking him to associate to it. "Tell me that again," or "How was that, exactly?" are not usually useful questions to ask about a dream. It has no "text" to be elicited and examined via associations. One has something better than a "text," one has the patient's first associations to it, and they are just as often valuable in dream analysis as his later associations will be. Sometimes they are more so. In any case they are not to be disregarded in an effort to clarify "the dream." They must be included among the associations that one hopes will lead to some understanding of the wishes and conflicts expressed in the dream.

To give an example, a young woman in analysis said,

"I had a dream last night, but I don't feel like telling it to you. It's kind of vague anyway. I think it was that my mother married my brother, sort of. It was something weird and stupid like that." She went on to say, "You'd think a dream like that would upset me, but I wasn't upset at all, that I can remember. It just seemed like, you know, ordinary."

The patient had nothing more to say about her dream, but if one views her account of it as her associations to her nocturnal experience, and if one has some knowledge of the analytic context of the dream, one can go a fair distance toward analyzing it. The context was this. The patient was angry with me because of a recent interruption to her treatment, an interruption to which she reacted as she had done in childhood when her father left on one of his frequent short business trips: it was another proof that he didn't love her as much as she wished, that she couldn't have him all for herself, and that he probably loved her mother and brother better than he loved her. Her way of dealing with her feelings of jealousy and resentment was to be very agreeable, very docile, very good, and, in particular, to convince herself and her father that she thought him the best, the wisest, and the most brilliant father who had ever lived. In her mind, to tell me a dream was to do me a great favor, to give me a chance to shine in her eyes. Just as she used to flatter her father by getting him to teach her something, she tried to overcome her anger at me by telling me a dream, even though she "didn't feel like it," so that I could show off by explaining what it meant to her. And what better gift could she offer than a dream of incest? What analyst wouldn't like a patient who brought him *such* a nice dream? After all, analysts think every patient wants to marry her father. It's everyday stuff to them or, as she put it, "ordinary." They don't even know how weird and stupid everyone thinks they are! But how could she dare talk to me that way? It would be too upsetting.

One can surmise, therefore, that during her sleep the patient had been angry and jealous. She wished she had me all to herself, that I had no other patients and no family but her. At the same time, she was angry at me and wanted to attack me and humiliate me as she felt humiliated by my not loving her as she wished me to. All of this was a repetition of, a transference from, her childhood feelings for her father. Neither her wish to have me for herself nor her wish to avenge herself on me could reach consciousness directly during her sleep. Both would have aroused too much anxiety. The former was repressed altogether. It must be guessed at from what she recalled of her dream. One must know that if a lonely, jealous little girl says, "Mama and Johnny should get married," what she really means is that they should go away together and never come back and she and Daddy will get married and he will stay with her forever. Her wish for revenge fared little better during her sleep, as far as one can judge from her account of the dream itself, but it came more into the open in her first associations, i.e., as she told her dream. It was given expression in, "I don't feel like telling it to you," "something weird and stupid" and "ordinary." Finally one may note that the very act of telling me her dream expressed her ambivalence. It was a reaction formation against her anger and at the same time a much watered-down expression of love.

Because of their frequency it is easy to find examples that demonstrate the value of keeping in mind the fact that a patient's account of a dream constitutes his first associations to it. For example, the following was told to me by chance as I was revising these pages.[1] A patient began an account of a dream by saying, "I have only some snatches of dreams today." What he went on to tell were accounts of dreams of the night before that had all to do with thoughts of women's genitals—in slang, women's snatches.

It is probably because too little explicit attention has been paid to the fact that a patient's report of a dream can be so useful in analyzing it that published reports of dreams in the analytic literature so rarely read like what one hears from patients in one's practice. So often it seems as though the meat of the dream is missing, that only its bare bones are on the page. Thus, e.g., the dream discussed above *in extenso* would, in all probability, usually be reported in one of two ways. It would read either, "The patient dreamed that her mother and brother were married," or, "The patient reported the following dream: 'My mother and brother were married.'" Either of these versions is perfectly accurate, but both omit much of what the patient actually said that was useful, even essential, in interpreting the dream. Both focus on what one assumes the patient experienced during her sleep rather than on what she said in reporting her experience. To do this, to focus on what a dreamer's conscious experience must have been during sleep while listening to his account of it during an analytic session, is to run the risk of neglecting what may be even more important clinically, i.e., the clues to the meaning of the dream that are contained in the account itself. It is this

[1] By Dr. W. Overholser.

account that is the stuff of dream analysis, not the analyst's reconstruction of the dream as he thinks the dreamer dreamed it.

Closely related to these considerations is the following. Case reports in the literature often contain accounts of dreams whose meaning is then stated without any of the patient's associations. The criticism that this amounts to wild analysis is not always quite correct. It leaves two facts out of account. First, that, as we have said, a patient's very account of a dream constitutes his first associations to it, and, second, that the more one knows about the dreamer, the more likely it is that one is able to understand the meaning of his dreams even without many further associations. Freud (1900) gave some examples of this in the children's dreams on pp. 127-131. When one knows very much about the psychological context in which a dream appears, as is often true in analysis, one can understand a good deal of the meaning of a dream as a patient tells it. One is surer of one's ground after one has heard his subsequent associations. Often they add much to one's understanding. But there may still be much that one has good evidence for even without them when a patient has been in analysis for quite some time.

One more point about dream analysis may be worth mentioning before we turn to other topics. Frequent reference has been made in the analytic literature to the dream as communication. In assessing the value of this idea about dreams, one must remember that when a patient is in analysis, every experience, every thought becomes something for him to communicate to his analyst. The wish to tell and the wish not to tell must be at least part of every patient's motivation all the time. The question is always, "How large a part is it this time?"

Every dream a patient remembers during analysis is a communication to his analyst. Every one has as part of its latent content a wish to communicate something. Conversely, every forgotten dream has as part of its latent content a wish not to tell something, and we know from the dream research of the last two decades that there are usually many forgotten dreams every night for each one that is remembered. Sometimes, as in the vignette above, a patient's wish to tell or not to tell a dream is of major psychological importance. When a patient, for example, is consciously greatly exercised over a need to tell his dreams, when he worries lest he forget one, when he debates with himself whether or not to write each one down so that he will "have something to analyze at least," it is clear that he is torn between a wish to tell and a wish not to do so, whatever purpose telling or not telling may serve in his psychic economy. In such a case an analyst's task is precisely to analyze both the wish to tell and the wish not to. For that patient, at that time in his analysis, the most important thing to analyze about any dream he may (or may not) tell is his motive for doing so.

Thus, for the patient in the vignette above, telling any dream was an expression of vitally important transference wishes, wishes that were in that case also represented in the manifest content of the dream itself. In fact, however, it was telling the dream that was the clearest representation of the most accessible, affectively significant derivatives of her oedipal wishes, i.e., of memories of asking her father to "explain something" to her. The analytic path to more deeply repressed oedipal derivatives necessarily led through an understanding and interpretation of the reasons for her feeling and behaving as she did about telling me any dream she had, i.e., about dreams as communications. And the same will be true whenever "to tell" or "not to tell," in however direct or disguised a form, stands in or close to the center of a patient's thoughts about any dream. If "to tell" is his main association, that is the most important thing to analyze. If it's not, then the "communicative function" of a dream can be safely assumed to be of no special importance and to call for no special analytic attention, even though it is, to be sure, omnipresent. It is obviously as unwise in analysis to emphasize unduly something that is of minor dynamic importance as it is to neglect something of major importance.

So much for the subject of dream analysis in the clinical setting. Let us turn our attention now to a different subject, that of the analysis of symptoms.

With rare exceptions a dream is a single incident in an analysis. It is reported, analyzed, and then superseded by new material. It is transient rather than lasting or even repetitive and it is properly treated in analysis as a transient phenomenon. There are exceptions—one or two dreams in an analysis that prove to be so revealing of important conflicts that they are referred to again and again by analyst or patient—but they are only exceptions. They are not the rule. A symptom, on the other hand, is a persistent or repeated evidence of psychic conflict rather than a transient one. In fact when a disturbing dream recurs night after night, as, for example, in patients with traumatic war neuroses, it is apt to be classified as a symptom for the very reason of its persistence.

The fact that symptoms are persistent gives one a certain advantage in analyzing them. They present themselves as objects of study again and again and often over a long period of time. One can observe repeatedly the psychic context in which they reappear as well as the context that is associated with their recession or disappearance. This information is often helpful in forming a conjecture about the nature and origins of the conflicts underlying a symptom, as the following vignette illustrates.

A woman in her early fifties had had many conversion symptoms throughout her adolescence and adult life. Moreover, she mistrusted and disliked doctors. None of them was any good, none could cure her, their medicines only made her worse. But on the few occasions when she had been seriously ill physically—a broken limb, an acute cholecystitis, profuse vaginal bleeding—she had been a changed woman. She became a sensible, cooperative, appreciative patient. Her conversion symptoms and her distrust of doctors disappeared. It should be added that her father had died when she was but two years old, and that her childhood was dominated by jealousy of her paternal cousins, whose fathers had lived, as well as by jealousy of boys and men in general.

From all of this one can conjecture that her hysterical symptoms were, at least in part, compromises between her wish to force the world to substitute for her lost father by treating her with special love and care and her need to punish herself for having such wishes. When she was physically ill, however, her conscience was clear. She need fear no more. She felt punished by her illness and could freely demand and enjoy the special care she was so guilty about wanting at other times.

There are forms of psychotherapy that focus exclusively on symptoms. By whatever different names they are called—conditioning, behavior modification, sex therapy—they have in common intentional neglect of the dynamics and history of the psychic conflicts of which symptoms are but one of the consequences. They focus only on the symptoms and they seek to cure symptoms, not to remove their cause. Analysis, by contrast, seeks to remove the cause of symptom formation by enabling a patient to deal better with the conflicts that caused his symptoms in the first place, with the result that his symptoms disappear along with the other improvements that take place in his mental life. For an analyst, what is of principal interest is the nature and origin of a patient's conflicts, not this or that symptom, i.e., this or that compromise formation.

There is no question of the correctness of this view. It is the whole of a patient's conflicts that must be focused on in analysis, not just one or another symptom. At the same time, one must remember that a symptom, like any other compromise formation, can lead to a better knowledge of the conflict of which it is a consequence if it can be analyzed. In this respect it is no different from a dream. Like dreams, symptoms are valuable in analysis as roads that can lead to a better understanding of a patient's conflicts.

Does an analyst, then, ask a patient to associate to symptoms as he asks him to associate to a dream? Certainly. There's no reason why he should not do so, as Lewin (1952) indicated. No reason in principle, that is. Just as in the case of a dream, there may be a good reason for not doing so now and then, but in general, one asks a patient to associate to a symptom, i.e., to talk about it as freely as possible. There is no better way to get to the meaning of a symptom, to reach some understanding of the conflicting forces in a patient's mind that have produced the symptom in question as a compromise among themselves.

Naturally one does not expect to achieve a thorough knowledge of the dynamics and genesis of a long-standing symptom or of the conflict of which it is a part either quickly or easily. Still, it is surprising how much one sometimes can surmise about a symptom rather soon. This is true, in all likelihood, for more than one reason. At least one important one is that many symptoms express childhood conflictual wishes in a rather direct and child-ish way. They are like naive or childhood dreams and fantasies in this respect. We all know how transparent and informative such fantasies are at times. For example, if a small boy says that he wishes his father would die so that he can have his gold watch, it is not difficult to guess at the incestuous, parricidal, and castrative wishes that gave rise to the child's fantasy. Note, by the way, that we're not considering whether the child can tolerate con-scious knowledge of those wishes—whether, if he is in analysis, any of them can be interpreted to him at the moment. All we're concerned with is our own conjecture or understanding of them. To continue with our analogy, some of the underlying wishes are equally evident if an adult patient reveals that he has never been able to keep a watch; that his father gave him a nice one when he graduated from high school, which he promptly broke; that he got another, even nicer, from his father when he finished college that he lost after a few weeks; and that a third watch came some years later as a Christmas present, also from his father, that he lost as well, so that now he buys only very cheap wristwatches for himself, keeps them for a year or so till they're worn out, and then buys a new one. Are not this patient's incestuous, parricidal, and castrative wishes as obviously involved in his symptomatic behavior as were those of the child in his fantasy? Indeed, the adult patient's symptomatic behavior tells us even more than does the child's fantasy, namely, that he is guilty and self-punitive about his oedipal wishes. And, we may add, no dream, early in analysis, would be likely to be more informative about a patient's conflicts than was this account of symptomatic behavior with watches.

To return to an earlier point, it is useful to keep in mind the point of view that one does not approach the analysis of a symptom expecting to "analyze" it fully in a single hour. One learns as much as one can from each attempt to analyze a patient's symptoms, knowing that one will never learn all that one would like to know at any one time. As another example of this, early in her analysis a young woman mentioned that she had been quite uncomfortable a couple of weeks before on the occasion of a trip to a bank. She had been invited to have lunch by a friend who worked there. When she arrived her friend took her to the lunch room. It was a windowless room below street level with but a single door. The patient felt anxious and had to excuse herself. I called to her attention that she had thought of this event just after telling me of her dead sister, who had died as a little girl, before the patient was born. Her sister's picture, the patient had told me, was kept on her dresser throughout her childhood. She always felt that her parents compared her unfavorably with her sister, that she was often bad while her sister had always been so good. "I hated her when I was growing up. I guess I was glad she was dead. Of course, if she hadn't died, I'd never have been born. Sometimes when I was little I wished I'd been the one who'd died instead of her."

The patient's response to my intervention was to say that she didn't see how an underground room could have reminded her of her dead sister, since her sister wasn't buried under the ground, but interred in a vault in a mausoleum, above ground level. "Of course," she added, "as we went into the dining room [in the bank] I saw that it was right next to the vault." She went on to say that she often became anxious in tunnels or in elevators, especially if traffic stopped in a tunnel so that one couldn't get out or if the elevator doors failed to open promptly.

It is apparent from this bit of symptom analysis that the patient's claustrophobia was at least in part a consequence of conflict over jealous and murderous wishes involving her sister and her parents. One can guess that a combination of "I hate her," "I wish I were her," "They'll hate me for hating her," and "Why do they go away? Why don't they come back and stay with me?" were all involved in the anxious fantasy of being entombed like her sister, mourned and beloved by parents who longed for her return, instead of the patient being lonely and longing for her parents to return, as had so often been the case during her childhood. It is equally apparent that this is far from a complete analysis of the symptom. It sheds no light, for example, on the patient's childhood fantasies about why her sister died, nor on her own oedipal wishes —her sister was five when she died—penis envy, and fantasies of anal birth. But it is a useful step, even though it's only a step, in the direction of a better understanding of the nature of the patient's conflicts and of their childhood origins.

A symptom often disappears in the course of analysis. Whenever it does so, one may be sure that its disappearance is the result of a shift in the balance among the derivatives of id, ego, and superego that make up the conflict of which the symptom is a compromise. The balance among these psychic elements may shift for many different reasons (Brenner, 1966, 1973b) — a "transference cure," a "flight to health," a change in a patient's life situation — but the shift I wish to consider here is that which comes about as a result of progress in analyzing a conflict. Substantial analytic progress necessarily brings about changes in the various compromise formations that are part of every patient's conflicts — in his neurotic symptoms, in his inhibitions, in his capacity for instinctual gratification, and in many of his character traits. When a symptom disappears as a result of analytic progress, its very disappearance is further evidence concerning the wishes and conflicts that were responsible for it in the first place.

For example, a woman in her thirties was anxious while flying in an airplane. She complained particularly of the fact that, should something go wrong, she was just a passenger. There was no way she could get to the controls and try to save the situation. Not that she could fly a plane herself. She had no experience whatever as a pilot. But the feeling of being unable even to get to the controls was somehow associated with great anxiety whenever she let herself dwell on it. Her further associations included the fact that on one occasion when she flew in a small, private plane she experienced no anxiety. She attributed this to the fact that there was at least a possibility for her "to do something" if necessary in a small plane, where she sat in the cockpit.

The nub of this patient's major conflicts was the fact that her younger sibling, her junior by four years, was a boy, while she "just a girl." She was partly furiously jealous, partly hopelessly dejected, and constantly guilty in consequence of what she unconsciously considered to be her castrated, inferior state. If one knows what the controls of an aircraft look like, it is easy to guess that for this patient, to sit at the controls of a plane with the control stick—which, incidentally, is colloquially known to pilots as the "joy stick," i.e., the penis—between her legs unconsciously gratified her wish to have a penis herself. Her conscious thought about being unable to get to the controls was understandable as the derivative or representative of two closely related unconscious ideas. The one was that if she were a man, if she had a penis, everything would be fine. She wouldn't have to be upset, because there would be no danger of anything terrible happening. The other unconscious idea was a wish to kill and castrate her brother, and, for that matter, her father as well, a wish that frightened her very much. To put things more connectedly, her symptom could be understood as follows. To fly a plane symbolized for the patient being a man with a penis. Being "just a passenger" symbolized being "just a girl," inferior and castrated. The anxiety she felt corresponded to the dangers—punishment and retributive genital injury—associated with her jealous, murderous, and castrative wishes, wishes that were stimulated whenever she had to be a passenger, while some man with that big stick between his legs flew the plane.

At the time she first told of her fear of flying, the patient was hardly conscious of jealousy of her brother, much less of being angry at him and wanting to have his penis for herself. She was conscious of some related ideas, for instance, bitterness over the fact that this is a man's world, in which women are but second-class citizens, but not of personal bitterness toward her brother. If anything, she was rather more protective toward him than he seemed to enjoy. As analysis progressed, she became more aware of the various elements of her penis envy: depressive affects, jealousy of brother and father, rage at them and at her mother, guilt and fear of abandonment, of genital injury, and of loss of love. Nothing more was heard of her fear of flying, and when she next flew, some months later, there was no mention of anxiety. The symptom disappeared as the conflict changed. The fact that it did so was additional confirmation that the symptom had really been part of the conflict it was attributed to.

Incidentally, this brief report also illustrates something about neurotic symptoms that is self-evident, in a way, and yet cannot be said too often. For an analyst to think of a patient as "a case of phobia," in this instance "of flight anxiety," does both himself and his patient a disservice. It is an incomplete and, hence, an inaccurate statement. Because it fails to do justice to the patient's symptom it may also impede the analytic work. Take the case of the patient just mentioned. A complete, accurate statement of her symptom would be that whenever she had to fly with nothing between her legs while a young man with whom she had no personal contact sat with a big stick between his legs and was the boss of the whole venture, she became anxious. When, however, she sat next to the man in charge, with something between her legs as well, she wasn't a bit frightened.

When her symptom is described in a way like this, in a way that really does it justice, one might react to the description by saying that she suffered from "flight anxiety" all right, but add that it was flight anxiety of a very special kind. True. But it's equally true that every patient's every symptom is "of a very special kind," just as every patient's every dream is unique. Generalizations are necessary and valuable in their proper place, but they have their limitations. When it comes to analyzing a patient's symptoms, what one wants to know are their individual, their unique features. Generalizations about symptoms are useful in calling attention to similarities among symptoms found in different patients. Being aware of such similarities may give one a useful hint about some of the elements of a patient's conflicts. At the same time one must remember that similar compromise formations are not always indicative of similar wishes and fears, just as one must remember that similar wishes and fears can give rise to very different compromise formations. In other words, such a hint must be used with caution. It should not be uncritically accepted as true for the case in hand simply because it is reported to have been true for others that seem on the surface to be similar.

The reminder that dissimilar symptoms can result from similar wishes and fears brings us to still another point that must always be kept in mind during one's clinical work. It, too, is familiar, but, like the last point, it bears repetition. When either infantile instinctual wishes or self-punitive and self-destructive tendencies or a combination of the two give rise to psychic conflicts of major proportions, the resulting compromise formations are never limited to one or several neurotic symptoms. There are always characterological consequences as well, some of them clearly pathological, the so-called neurotic character disturbances, some well within normal limits, and others that are hard to label with certainty as normal or pathological. In other words, a patient's symptoms are never isolated phenomena. Their dynamic bases and their origins are always closely related to those of other important compromise formations of the same individual. We are accustomed to making a distinction between character neuroses and symptom neuroses, but perhaps the distinction is less important than it has often been supposed to be. In years gone by, when the emphasis in diagnosis was on whether a patient was suffering from conversion symptoms, or from anxiety and phobias, or from obsessions and compulsive rituals, characterological problems were usually noted only after analysis had begun and as they surfaced in the course of treatment. More recently diagnostic emphasis is likely to be focused on characterological problems during the initial interviews, so that not infrequently it is a patient's symptoms that come into focus only as analysis progresses. To complicate things still further, patients' complaints — not what they suffer from, but what they complain of — tend to go by fashion, so that young adults may complain of a sense of alienation, lack of purpose or goals, and disinterest in life — the fashion, that is — and only after some time does it appear that a patient with such complaints is using a stereotype to conceal from himself even more than from his analyst the symptoms and characterological problems from which he really suffers. In other words, complaining à la mode can be a patient's way of reassuring himself that he's not as ill and as different from his fellows as he fears himself to be.

The main point is, however, that symptoms are not isolated phenomena in a patient's life. They are part of an organic whole, part of the totality of his mental life. Whatever may be the compromise formations that result from an individual's psychic conflicts, the ones that we call symptoms are as much a part of the person as are all the others. In fact they differ from normal compromise formations rather in degree than in kind (Brenner, 1973a, Chapters 8 and 9). Incidentally, one might add what is obvious from this discussion, i.e., that a symptom is never "a defense." In any compromise formation defenses play an important part, but, by definition, never more than a part. Homosexuality does not "defend against" schizophrenia, nor do obsessional symptoms ward off depression. Such formulae are much too simple to do justice to the facts.

But to return to our main theme, one should always remember that a symptom or, for that matter, a neurotic character disturbance, is part of how a patient thinks, feels, and behaves when he is rejected, when he is loved, when he is lonely, when he is part of a crowd, when he has failed or succeeded, when he is sexually excited, when he is inhibited, or frightened, or angry, when he feels frustrated or gratified, as the case may be. Like any other psychic phenomenon, a symptom fits into a patient's life. However long-standing and repetitive it may be, its appearance or intrusion into a patient's consciousness is each time a result of what the patient was thinking and experiencing at the moment, just as every dream, whatever its infantile latent content, has some reference to and is in some degree the result of events of the moment in the dreamer's life. It isn't quite correct to think, as we so often do, of a neurotic symptom as something distinct from the organized, integrated, and normal part of a patient's ego.

For instance, a patient complains of recurrent backache, or headache, or stomachache. "Analyzing his symptom" means much more than asking what comes to his mind about it. Such associations "to his symptom" are not to be neglected or ignored. Whatever a patient may say deserves attention. The words he uses to describe a symptom are, after all, his first associations to it and are often for that reason of special importance, just as is the report of a dream (see above). But what is being emphasized here is the importance in symptom analysis of learning as much as can be learned of the psychological context in a patient's life in which a symptom appeared or, as is frequently the case, the context in which it reappeared. It is very useful to learn, if one can, about a particular episode of pain, the one that occurred yesterday, today, or over the weekend, maybe. What a patient was doing, thinking, or feeling when he noticed the pain, what he thought of when he felt it, etc., very often furnish valuable clues to the unconscious conflicts of which the symptom—in this case, of pain—is a part.

Not that patients should be quizzed about their symptoms, any more than about their dreams or anything else. Spontaneous expression is obviously the ideal. But when a patient consistently omits details of the sort just mentioned and talks of his symptoms only in generalities like, "I always feel faint in a crowded bus," or "It's the take-off that makes me nervous every time," one can be sure that he is avoiding the details for a reason, usually an unconscious one. This should be brought to his attention, and one should attempt to analyze it like any other important resistance.

It is when a patient's resistance is not too strong, when he is able to talk freely about a symptomatic episode, that one can see most clearly the relationship between his symptom and the other aspects of his life that are dynamically related compromise formations. For instance, the patient who was anxious when flying, as described above, had a recurrence of the symptom on one occasion after she had been free of it for many months. The obvious question was, "What was it that had precipitated her relapse?" As she talked about the episode, she remembered that when she was anxious she had, as she expressed it, "an empty feeling in my stomach. A real sick feeling." She couldn't remember the last time she'd been sick to her stomach. She paused for several seconds, then proceeded with obvious reluctance. The last time she could remember was when she had performed fellatio on her boy-friend at his request. She hadn't enjoyed it at all. She had felt humiliated and used. It had made her sick to her stomach. On the plane, she said, she didn't eat a thing. She just passed up the meal altogether. Luckily she'd had a good lunch earlier in the day. She'd gone to a special place with a fellow worker and had had two large boiled sausages, which was sort of a treat for her. She used to love them when she was a girl, but has eaten them infrequently as an adult.

It must be added that the flight in question was part of a business trip. She had just been promoted to a position of greater responsibility and was flying to a conference as a result. It should also be added that to be promoted meant to her that her chief, an older man, preferred her to her colleagues, many of whom were men, something she equated, though at first only unconsciously, with having her father prefer her to her brother, who had been a principal rival in her childhood and a chief object of her jealousy.

I hope that this brief account will serve to persuade the reader of what was abundantly substantiated by the analytic material, namely, that being in a plane en route to the conference after her recent promotion symbolized unconsciously the gratification of frightening, guilt-laden wishes. It meant to her that she had triumphed over her brother by biting off his penis, that she had it now, and that she was the favored sibling, the boy in the family. For this crime she had to pay, and pay she did with anxiety, nausea, hunger, and disgust with herself for being such a "sissy" as to be frightened by flying. But what is of particular interest in the context of our present discussion is to note that the same childhood wishes — to be a boy and her father's favorite — that resulted in her symptom had equal relevance to other aspects of her adult life. For example, they influenced her choice of vocation, and they accounted for much of the pleasure she got from her work, as well as for inhibitions and unhappiness in connection with it. In a very real sense, then, this patient's symptom, on the occasion just described, was part of her reaction to her promotion. It is equally true that one cannot understand the symptom without reference to the patient's unconscious conflicts and to their origins in the instinctual wishes and fears of her childhood. It is this fact, indeed, that has been most emphasized by analysts, beginning with Freud himself, in their elucidation of the psychology of neurotic symptoms. What is helpful to keep in mind during one's clinical work is that each time a symptom reappears it is because something in the present has activated the childhood instinctual conflict of which the symptom is a result. The "something" may be, as in this case, a change in the patient's life situation. It may be a sexual experience. It may be what's happening in analysis, in particular, something in the transference, and so on. Whatever the reason, the past has become active in the present as a neurotic symptom, just as it is continually and repeatedly active in the present in so many ways. One must bear in mind that a symptom is one of those many ways. It is different from the others in certain respects, but never entirely divorced from them, and, what is of practical importance, its connection with the other aspects of a patient's life can furnish important clues to the understanding of the conflicts that underlie them all.

So much for symptoms and their importance for analytic technique. There is another feature of mental life that is also valuable as a way of learning about the nature and origins of a patient's psychic conflicts. It is what is included under the heading of daydreams, conscious fantasies, or reverie. It properly includes both personal fantasies, i.e., fantasies unique to a patient, and ready-made or communal ones like films, plays, TV, fiction, poetry, myths, and religious beliefs. As in the case of symptoms, it is surprising how little has been written that deals specifically with analyzing such conscious fantasies in a clinical setting. Not that they have been ignored or undervalued as to their importance for mental life. There are many books and articles on religion, mythology, and literature, for example, and the importance of daydreams was recognized very early in the development of psychoanalysis (e.g., Freud, 1908). Yet their proper role in psychoanalytic technique is important enough to deserve even more extensive and explicit attention than they have, in general, received. The subject is one that should receive special attention in courses on psychoanalytic technique, perhaps with particular emphasis on masturbatory and related sexual fantasies.

In principle the analytic approach to an element of waking fantasy life is the same as the approach to a symptom or a dream, i.e., to learn as much as possible of its determinants and connections in a patient's psychic life from his associations to it and from the context in which it appears. It is important that a fantasy not be taken at face value, e.g., simply as a connected story. This is especially true when one is dealing with a play or a work of fiction. Neither the author's intention nor the analyst's own reaction is of chief importance. It is the patient's associations that occupy this position in analysis. The same is true for any other shared or communal fantasy, like a myth or religious belief. The same fantasy can have very different meanings to different individuals. There are even those to whom the principal significance of Sophocles' *King Oedipus* appears to be the theme of hostility between mother and son (Levin, 1957) and others to whom it seems to be filicide (Rascovsky and Rascovsky, 1968).

A brief digression may be to the point here. No work of art, whatever its nature, has a meaning in and of itself. To speak of "the meaning" of any work of art can make sense only if what is meant is its full significance, conscious and unconscious, to certain individuals. There are some stories, myths, and religious legends whose relation to the common instinctual wishes and conflicts of childhood is direct and unambiguous. *The Brothers Karamazov* is about parricide. So are *Jack and the Beanstalk*, and Sophocles' *King Oedipus*. Whatever childhood wishes and conflicts any of the three is connected with in a male patient's mind, those about parricide must be among them. Each patient's conflicts about parricide are unique, to be sure. They can be discovered only with the help of his associations and the knowledge his associations bring of the details of his early experiences. But what one learns is bound to concern parricide in one way or another. Most stories and myths, however, are ambiguous. They have a multiple appeal and can "mean" quite different things to different people. The more intricate the plot and the less clear it is, the more likely is this to be so. In most cases, therefore, attempts to apply psychoanalytic knowledge to the "understanding" of a work of fiction or of a fictional character are unconvincing for the reason that they are misdirected. There is not one "meaning" that is valid for everyone. There are many "meanings," each valid for some but none valid for all.

In addition, there are times when one's psychic state is such that one preoccupation overshadows everything else. Every patient becomes at times a person with but one thing, whatever it may be, on his mind. When this is so, his associations to a work of art, as to anything else, will concern mainly one or another aspect of the topic that is so completely engrossing to him for the moment.

Thus one is dependent on a patient's associations in trying to reach a valid conjecture about the meaning to him of any story or myth. What a story or myth means to ninety-nine other persons is no guarantee of its meaning to the hundredth. This is true partly because of the ambiguous nature of most such works of art and partly because of the powerful influence on thought and perception that is exerted by intense conflicts, unconscious though they may be.

When it comes to analyzing a patient's own, personal daydreams, no clinical example can surpass the one Freud supplied in "Screen Memories" (1899). For many years it was not readily accessible because Freud suppressed it after its original publication for reasons of discretion. It has been easily available since the publication of the *Standard Edition* of his works, however, and it well repays reading and study. It may be noted that

Freud called what he analyzed a memory, rather than a fantasy, but it seems equally appropriate to consider it an adolescent's fantasy of his childhood, one feature of which was a conviction that it really happened.

Fantasies not infrequently appear during the course of an analytic hour. For example, a young man, in the course of talking about the monthly analytic bill he had just received, imagined putting his fist through the panel of my office door. He laughed at the idea of there being a hole in the door. "What would you say to your other patients?" he went on. "You wouldn't be able to see patients at all till the door was fixed. So I was thinking in my mind that I would pay you. Not just for the door, that I'd pay, that I'd have to pay for all the time you couldn't see patients till it was fixed."

Thus the patient's associations led to his jealousy of my other patients, a subject of which he had previously spoken but rarely, and even then with no feeling of conviction that he was jealous of them. It was, in fact, the imminence of a summer holiday that had reminded him unconsciously of the many times in his childhood when his parents were absent from home and he was left in the care of a nursemaid. She, like me, cared for him for money, not for love, and, like me, her attention was divided among the several children who were left in her care. It was difficult for him to think that he had ever been angry at his nursemaid. She had been the person he had loved the most intensely as a child. His worst nightmares as a little boy had been of her death.

All that could be appropriately interpreted to the patient at the time was the revival in the transference of the childhood feelings and wishes just described. It is not hard to conjecture in addition an unconscious sadistic fantasy of intercourse, symbolized by the image of smashing a hole in my door. This conjecture was supported by other facts, such as adolescent sexual fantasies and a number of features of his adult sexual relations with women. In addition, analysis of the fantasy contributed evidence in favor of a genetic hypothesis, namely, that his wish to be cruel to women sexually was motivated in part by his wish to revenge himself on both his mother and his nursemaid for deserting him so often and, in particular, for having, as he felt, neglected him when his younger sibling was born.

A slip of the tongue during an hour, the use of a striking phrase or metaphor, or a joke a patient tells may also be a useful source of information about the nature and origins of a patient's conflicts when it can be analyzed, i.e., when a patient can associate to it. A word of caution must be added here, however. In principle jokes, metaphors, slips, conscious fantasies, dreams, and symptoms are all something worth having a patient associate to. In practice one must beware of seeming to insist to a patient that he associate to every one that comes up in the course of an hour. To do so involves too great a risk of interfering with the patient's spontaneous course of associations and of imposing upon him one's own ideas of what he should be thinking and talking about.

It is part of good analytic technique, I believe, to acquaint patients at some time fairly early in their analysis with the fact that it is useful to analyze all of these psychic phenomena. I may add that this need not even be done in so many words. One can make the matter clear simply by asking a patient for his associations as suitable occasions arise. What usually happens then is that patients themselves associate to the phenomena in question as they appear in the analytic material. If they consistently or conspicuously fail to do so, there is always a reason for it, and the reason is usually either defensive, a consequence of transference, or a combination of the two. What is indicated in such a case is that one call to a patient's attention that he is avoiding talking about whatever it is that he's avoiding, not that one instruct him, however tactfully, to mend his ways, analytically speaking. The decision about one's course of action in such an instance, as in every similar instance, should be guided by one's awareness of the nature of the analytic task as a whole—the task of understanding as fully as possible the nature and origins of each patient's psychic conflicts. Whatever one thinks is likely to serve this purpose best is what one should do. Any personal bias will inevitably influence the transference, whether the bias is in favor of dreams or of anything else in the analytic material. In the long run it is more useful to avoid the effects of such a bias, in my opinion, than it is to analyze this or that dream, symptomatic manifestation, etc.

SUMMARY

1. Substantial advantages accrue from revising the theory of the psychology of dreams along the lines Arlow and I (1964) have suggested.

2. What is usually thought of as the manifest content of a dream is not really that. It is, rather, an account that represents a patient's first associations to his dream. Recognition of this fact entails practical advantages for one's analytic work.

3. One can often understand a good deal of the meaning of the dream of a patient who has been in analysis for some time simply from his account of it without further associations.

4. Whatever a patient dreams while in analysis is related to his desire to communicate with his analyst. So is everything else a patient tells or withholds in analysis. The importance of the wish to communicate and withhold varies from dream to dream. It may or may not be of principal or major importance.

5. The traditional emphasis on the importance of dreams in psychoanalytic therapy has been at the expense of attention to the place in analysis of such other mental phenomena as daydreams, slips, metaphors, jokes, reactions to works of art and even neurotic symptoms. All of them are, like dreams, compromise formations. All, under suitable circumstances, can contribute significantly to an understanding of the nature and origins of the psychic conflicts of which each is a part.

6. Illustrations are offered of the value of analyzing symptoms in psychoanalysis. The reader's attention is drawn to the significance for analytic work of the persistent and/or repetitive nature of symptoms. The meanings of disappearance and/or reappearance of symptoms are discussed with illustrations.

7. A symptom, like a dream, is unique in every instance. Superficially similar symptoms can result from dissimilar conflicts; similar conflicts can give rise to superficially dissimilar symptoms.

8. In analyzing a symptom it is always useful and often essential to pay attention to the psychic context in which it appears.

9. A patient's account of a symptom, like his account of a dream, contains his first associations to it.

10. A symptom is never merely a defense. It is a compromise in which defenses play a part.

11. Symptoms are not isolated phenomena. They

are part of an organic whole, part of the totality of a patient's mental life. The relation between a symptom and other aspects of a patient's life, both normal and pathological, can furnish important clues to an understanding of the conflicts that underlie all of them.

12. No work of art, whatever its nature, has a meaning in and of itself. It makes sense to speak of "the meaning" of a work of art only if one uses the word to refer to its significance, conscious or unconscious, to one or more persons. There is not one "meaning" that is valid for everyone. There are many "meanings," each valid for some but none valid for all.

13. An illustration is offered of the value of analyzing a daydream. In addition, the reader is referred to an exceptionally instructive example in the literature (Freud, 1899).

7

GOALS OF ANALYSIS, CASE SELECTION, PRACTICAL ARRANGEMENTS, AND OTHER TOPICS

As its title indicates, this chapter is devoted to a discussion of a somewhat miscellaneous group of subjects. The first three—the goals of analysis, selection, and termination—do form a single topic in certain respects, since all depend to an important extent on the possibility of altering a patient's psychic conflicts by means of analysis. The four final ones, however, have no special relationship to one another or to the first three except as they have all to do with aspects of psychoanalytic technique.

Some of the topics of this chapter have been discussed extensively either in the literature, by word of mouth, or both. Others have had relatively little attention paid them. A great deal has been written on the subject of termination, for example. Less has been written about selecting cases for analysis, but very much has been said about it in institute seminars, at intake committee meetings, and at innumerable case conferences. Practical arrangements, on the other hand, are not a subject that has been much talked about or thought about, with one exception. At the beginning of his career, when he is starting with his first cases, nearly every analyst tends to focus some of his anxiety about doing analysis at last on just what to say about practical arrangements to each new patient and how to say it. And if practical arrangements have attracted but little attention, the goals of analysis have received even less, at least in any systematic or general way. The question of limited goals for a particular patient will often come up for discussion, but only rarely the question of what the goals of analysis are for patients in general. (For an excellent review of the subject see Wallerstein, 1965. See also Ticho, 1972.)

It is to be expected that there will be little new to say about the topics that have been discussed most often and most extensively by others in the past. All that one can expect to be able to do with them is to add some details or to suggest a fresh way of looking at familiar facts. In consequence the topics that have less often been discussed will receive the fuller treatment simply because there is more to be said about them that isn't already well known to most readers.

Our first topic is the goals of analysis. What are they? Or, better, how are they to be defined?

Should the definition be a therapeutic one, with the emphasis on the cure of symptoms and the relief of suffering? Should it be in terms of the analytic process and emphasize rather self-knowledge, or perhaps even the development in the analysand of an ability to analyze himself after his "analysis" is over? Or an ethically oriented definition that lays stress on emotional growth and on an ability to realize to the fullest extent one's potential as a human being? Or perhaps a hedonistic one according to which the principal goal would be to achieve the capacity both for "full" instinctual gratification and for pleasurable and rewarding sublimation? No one will question the fact that each of these is often the result of a successful analysis, but which of them is its legitimate goal and which is but a welcome by-product?

In any attempt to answer this question, one must keep in mind the following considerations. Each of the definitions of the goals of analysis that has just been suggested refers implicitly to one or another type of psychological difficulty—to symptoms and suffering, to ignorance of one's own wishes and fears, to too little self-reliance or self-sufficiency, to an inhibition of psychic development with consequent psychic immaturity, and to instinctual inhibitions. Psychic conflicts that originate in connection with infantile instinctual wishes can be responsible for any or all of the difficulties alluded to. Such conflicts give rise to those compromise formations that we identify as neurotic symptoms, to mental suffering, to a downright refusal to admit one's own wishes and fears even to oneself, to an inability to develop one's capacities to their fullest extent, to inadequate object and sexual relationships, to defects in sublimation, and to an inability to enjoy life fully. Insofar as any such difficulty is due to psychic conflict, its disappearance or improvement is a legitimate goal of psychoanalysis. Which is the more important goal and which is merely an incidental one will depend mainly on the individual circumstances of the case. For one patient the difficulties caused by his conflicts will be mainly of one sort, for another they will be of a different sort. The analytic goals will, therefore, vary from case to case in accordance with the consequences of conflict in each. At the same time it is obvious that the same general formulation applies to all. In every case the goal of psychoanalysis is to alter a patient's psychic conflicts in such a way as to eliminate or alleviate their adverse effects. The results of such an alteration will appear as symptomatic and characterological changes, as an improved potential for "growth," as better object relations, as more pleasure, as less misery, etc. It is, in fact, just this relationship between symptomatic and characterological difficulties on the one hand and alterations in conflicts of infantile instinctual origin on the other that is the best proof that there is a causal connection between the two.

The goal of analysis, then, is to alter a patient's psychic conflicts so as to produce a beneficial result. What the beneficial result will be will depend on what the symptomatic and otherwise detrimental results of the patient's conflicts were in the first place. We have already been reminded in our discussion of symptom analysis that an important conflict never has a single result in mental functioning. A symptom is never a solitary phenomenon. Important conflicts always have a widespread and manifold influence on mental functioning and, for that matter, on mental development as well, since such conflicts begin in early childhood at a time when mental development is still proceeding actively. Clearly, therefore, the effects of conflict on a patient's mental life and behavior must be many and varied.

A necessary consequence of this is that when analysis

is successful in altering conflict, the beneficial results are widespread. If, for example, a patient has major conflicts over infantile competitive, castrative, and murderous wishes concerning his brother, he will, in the course of analysis, become gradually less frightened by them, less guilty about them, and more able to tolerate conscious awareness of them. In other words, analysis will result in an alteration of his conflict. As it does so, improvement will be observable not just in one, but in a number of aspects of his mental functioning. Although the patient may have complained only of sexual difficulties with women, perhaps, improvement will not be limited to the symptom of which he complained. There will be improvement as well in whatever other areas of functioning had been adversely affected by that particular conflict, with the result that the patient may become capable of better academic achievement, for example, or he may compete better in sports, his capacity for aesthetic pleasure may be heightened, his moods may be more stable, he may lose a somatic symptom that had been troubling him, etc. Some of these may be expected or predictable. Others come as a surprise as much to the analyst as to the patient, or they may even go unnoticed as such for weeks or months, but all are the result of alteration of conflict by analysis. It's like what happens when one cuts the main stem of a vine that has grown so that for years its leaves have mingled with those of the tree that supports it. Only as its leaves wither and turn brown can one see how widely the vine has spread among the branches of its host and to what unsuspected places it has grown.

It may be objected that improvement in mental functioning does not always follow on analysis of conflict. "I've interpreted that to my patient, but it didn't do any good," or words to that effect, are not uncommonly heard when a patient is being discussed whose analytic progress has been less than satisfactory. Why has the analyst's understanding, conveyed to his patient by interpretation, failed to produce the expected and desired result?

This is a question to which no general answer can be given. We shall leave to one side the possibility that the analyst's understanding of the case, or his interpretation, or both, were incorrect, incomplete, or otherwise faulty. In such a case no further explanation is necessary for the patient's lack of progress. Instead I shall repeat what I wrote in Chapter 2 about the alterations that one can expect in analytic work. As Freud (1914) was the first to recognize, it is not reasonable to expect that a single interpretation, however complete, will effect very much change in a major conflict. Something with enough potential for terror and misery to have affected large areas of a person's mental functioning for the better part of his lifetime is not going to yield that quickly and that easily. What one observes under the best of circumstances is an extended period of gradual change, marked by the ebb and flow of improvement and relapse. Occasionally there will be a dramatic change for the better, but, as we have observed before, such changes have always been preceded by a long period of preparation and we may add here that they rarely persist for very long without some evidence of relapse into the *status quo ante*.

One should remember, therefore, that dissatisfaction with a patient's analytic progress and doubt about the efficacy of one's interpretations may sometimes be due to an insufficient appreciation of the fact that progress in analysis is never more than slow, always inter-

mittent, and invariably interrupted by relapses. As one of
the examples in Chapter 6 illustrates, even relapses can
be useful analytically and the same is true for a period of
apparent stagnation. The analyst's constant question:
"Why?" is applicable to everything he can observe about
his patient. If a patient makes progress, one tries as an
analyst to understand in what ways his conflicts have
changed to make that progress possible and, if one can,
to understand what analytic and other influences made
for the change. The same if he fails to make progress or if
he relapses. The ideal in every instance is to form as
reliable a conjecture as possible, i.e., to understand what
is going on and why. Often one can do so very well. When
that is the case even a relapse is not a matter for concern.
It is merely something new to analyze—more analytic
material, more grist for the mill. When one cannot understand so well, one must revise or enlarge one's conjectures or understanding of the patient's relevant conflicts
to fit the new facts and to offer a satisfactory explanation
of them.

Thus a patient's apparent lack of progress in analysis, his apparent unresponsiveness to interpretations, can
be due to one or more than one of several causes. Like
any other aspect of his speech or behavior, it is a proper
object of analytic scrutiny and understanding.

But what of the final goal of analysis as therapy?
When is an analysis finished? More modestly, when
should it be terminated? Or, to put the matter in other
words, how much should one expect to be able to alter a
patient's psychic conflicts for the better?

Once again it must be confessed that a satisfactory
general answer is impossible. Each case has special features that require individual consideration. Obviously

one's experience with other cases is important, as is the experience of colleagues with whom one may discuss one's cases, either on a formal or an informal basis. Only one thing is certain: the decision is always a matter of judgment. It is a question of balancing pros and cons. Symptoms often disappear as a result of successful analytic work. Characterological and other problems may do likewise. But psychic conflict that results from infantile instinctual wishes never disappears. It cannot do so. It is, as I have repeatedly emphasized (see Brenner, 1973a, Chapter 9), as important a part of normal mental life as it is of what we label pathological in mental functioning. If we know anything about the mind of man, we know that psychic conflicts can only be altered, either by analysis or by any other means. They can never be eradicated.

In every case, therefore, the goal of analysis is a limited one. It is to achieve the greatest degree of beneficial alteration of psychic conflict that one can achieve in that particular case by analytic means. As soon as one feels that he has a fairly good understanding of an analytic patient, i.e., as soon as one's conjectures about his psychic conflicts begin to take shape, one tries to guess how much he can expect to alter those conflicts in analysis. First guesses will usually be tentative. Any guess is subject to revision as the analytic work proceeds. But some guess one is bound to make, whether consciously or unconsciously. Indeed such a guess is an important part of evaluating a patient in order to decide whether to recommend analysis in the first place, a topic that we shall turn to in a moment.

We should not leave the subject of the goals of analysis, however, without explicit reference to the knowledge, gained from experience with analysis, that the degree of alteration of psychic conflict that a successful analysis can compass is enough to be of immense practical importance in a patient's life. It can make the difference between crippling inhibition and successful functioning, between misery and happiness, or between life and death. Important as it is to realize that analysis cannot do what is impossible, i.e., eradicate or eliminate psychic conflict, it is equally important to realize the great value of what analysis can do. To realize its limitations is not to say that what it can do is of little value. On the contrary, it is of such great value that if there is a good chance of achieving it, it is well worth all the time, the effort, and the expense that analysis entails.

This brings us then to the problems involved in the selection of cases for analysis. How does one decide whether or not to recommend analysis to a particular patient?

The answer to this question involves the consideration of many and varied factors (see Waldhorn, 1960; Tyson and Sandler, 1971). It is obvious that such factors as geography, time, money, or other external circumstances may determine what advice one gives to a patient about starting analysis. These, and any one of a host of other factors, may help one to decide in a particular case whether a patient is likely to profit from analysis or whether he is unlikely to (Waldhorn, 1960).

Every analyst not only has access to the literature on case selection, he also necessarily participates over and over again in discussions about individual patients' suitability for analysis. He must inevitably make his own decision in many cases, must advise others in making theirs, and must be advised by them. I do not believe that a book like this can add substantially to the list of factors that analysts are accustomed to take into consideration in selecting a case for analysis rather than for some other form of therapy. I do think it useful, however, to point out that many of the factors that are customarily considered can be grouped under the general heading of psychic conflict, since they are in fact elements or consequences of conflict.

When one applies what has just been said about the goals of analysis to the situation of evaluating a patient's suitability for analysis, it is evident that a part of any such evaluation is an attempt to decide what the likelihood is that that patient's conflicts can be understood and beneficially altered by analysis. In other words, one attempts to assess in advance the goals of analysis for the prospective patient and to decide, on the basis of one's assessment, whether analysis is worthwhile. Neither assessment nor decision is ever completely certain and reliable. In the best of cases some little doubt will remain and in most, a considerable degree of doubt. All that can be said is that decision is more likely to be reliable if one applies to the task of evaluation one's analytic knowledge of the importance of conflict in mental life, i.e., of the relation of conflict to every aspect of a patient's conscious thought and behavior. Whatever one knows or observes about a patient, whether it be normal or pathological, past or present, thought or behavior — in a word, whatever it is — is a compromise formation and, as such, a clue to the patient's psychic conflicts. Within the limits of the situation one will use all the clues one has in one's efforts to delineate as much as one can of the nature of the conflicts, or their severity, i.e., the degree to which they have handicapped or crippled the patient, and, if possible, something of their origins. In a given case one may be limited to such conclusions as, e.g., that conflicts over aggression bulk large, as witness the patient's sadomasochistic fantasies, her need to be always kind and good, and her choice of poverty law as a profession. Or in another case, that the patient's sexual and other problems in her relations with men seem likely to be related to the fact that her father and mother were divorced when she was four and that her stepfather deserted her mother and herself when she was eighteen. Or in another that denial seems to play a large role in the patient's defenses, and so on. The point is, simply, that complaints, symptoms, overt behavior, traits of character, style of dress, life history, and whatever else, are all to be used as data that furnish the basis for a preliminary conjecture or understanding of one or another aspect of each patient's psychic conflicts. What one tries to do, in effect, is to fit them all together.

When the task of evaluation is viewed in this way such questions as the prognostic significance of one or another symptom, the relative importance of this or that character trait, whether a patient has a "symptom neurosis" or a "character neurosis," and the like, appear in better perspective. All such questions are seen to be subordinate to the more general one raised here concerning a patient's conflicts, since all the psychic phenomena they refer to — symptoms, character traits, etc. — are components of conflict or consequences of it. Even the question of "an intact ego" as a prerequisite for recommending analysis can be better phrased and correspondingly better understood in the terms suggested here. No one's ego is "intact" in the sense of being uninfluenced by conflict or uninvolved in it. On the contrary, normal compromise formations are as much a part of conflict and as firmly rooted in it as pathological ones are. In addition, many aspects of ego functioning are normally quite infantile (Brenner, 1968a), much more so than is often explicitly recognized in the analytic literature, at least. "Intactness" of ego functioning is never more than a relative matter, and the truth is that patients whose egos are called intact are those whose symptoms are comparatively few and mild, whereas patients who are said to lack an intact ego are those whose symptoms are numerous and severe. If other things are equal, a patient whose psychic conflicts have resulted in many severely crippling compromise formations will naturally be expected to have a poorer prognosis than another whose compromise formations are less crippling and less disruptive of his life.

To repeat what cannot be said too often, one must be both cautious and modest in assessing a patient for the purpose of recommending analysis. It is difficult to make an assessment on the basis of what is nearly always very limited information. Granting all the necessary reservations, however, I believe that many of the relevant facts are best understood in terms of their relationship to the patient's psychic conflicts, that they should be used as clues to the nature, origin, and intensity of those conflicts, and that one should always ask and at least try to answer the question, "How much can one expect to understand this patient's conflicts and to alter them beneficially by analysis?"

The same question is an analyst's best guide in deciding about termination of analysis. If analysis has been at all successful, he is in a much better position to formulate a reliable answer to it when it is time to think about termination than he was at or before the start of analysis. The time must necessarily come when it seems to an analyst that his patient's conflicts have been beneficially altered as much as they are ever likely to be altered by analysis. Whether or not the patient reaches the same conclusion at about the same time, it is the analyst's responsibility to make his own decision and to present it as such to his patient. If both are in agreement, so much the better.

There is not, or, at any rate, there should not be any stereotype or formula that an analyst uses in telling a patient that he thinks he is ready to terminate his analysis. The special circumstances of the transference will nearly always dictate the most appropriate way in which to convey one's decision to a patient. Similar considerations will influence the decision as to when the termination date is best set, though it should be noted that analysts are generally agreed that the date should be far enough in the future to give both analyst and patient an opportunity to analyze the latter's reactions to terminating.

Often, as many authors have emphasized, a patient reacts to termination primarily as to the loss of an important object—a mourning reaction, as it is usually called. This is by no means always the case, however, as Arlow and I have shown (Arlow and Brenner, 1966). Whatever the reaction may be—and for most patients it is a mixed one—it should be analyzed as thoroughly as possible. One can be sure, also, that transference wishes and their consequences will figure prominently in the analytic material.

Little more need be added here on the subject of termination, but perhaps a word is in order about what is sometimes referred to as "forced termination," i.e., setting a termination date as a device for ending a period of analytic stagnation and forcing a patient to analyze, willy-nilly. Freud (1918) did this with one of his patients, the Wolf Man. In that case it seemed to work brilliantly, although it must be admitted that the patient's subsequent course (Brunswick, 1928) was far from satisfactory. At any rate, Freud (1918) expressed his reservations about the procedure even when he first reported using it and it has not seemed to be very often useful in other hands. At the present time there would seem to be better ways of dealing with a period of stagnation than by putting a peremptory end to the analysis. If analysis of the factors responsible for the continued lack of analytic progress is unsuccessful in altering a patient's conflicts, one must at least wonder whether as much progress has been achieved as it is possible to achieve with that particular patient. If so, it is usually best to suggest termination or, if one prefers to call it so, an interruption of analysis in the usual way.

The next subjects to be considered in this chapter are those that come under the heading of practical arrangements. These are an inevitable part of every psychoanalytic situation (Arlow and Brenner, 1966) and as such they are familiar to every analyst. He acquaints his patient with most of them at the start of analysis, in fact, and they usually remain unchanged throughout its course: the couch, the position of the analyst out of his patient's range of vision, the appointment schedule, fee schedule, method of payment, etc. Such matters are largely dealt with in a routine way. They have evoked relatively little interest and discussion among analysts—probably less than their actual importance deserves.

Let us begin by raising a question about the most nearly universal of them: can one analyze a patient who isn't lying down on a couch in such a position that he can't see his analyst? Must a patient "use the couch" for it to be real analysis? The advantages to both patient and analyst of the conventional arrangement are so substantial as to have made it pretty universally the arrangement of choice. The question is whether it is a necessity as well, or whether it can be either altered or dispensed with altogether in some instances. It is a question that can best be answered with the help of some illustrative case material.

First of all consider a patient who at the very start made it a condition of her treatment that she not be required to lie down on the couch. When asked her thoughts about her request, she replied that she'd been told that one of the things about psychoanalysis is that every patient has to fall in love with her analyst. This, she went on, was something she wasn't going to do. I said to her that it seemed as though she felt that lying down on the couch was the same as falling in love with me, and added, "I guess you think that if you agree to lie down it's the same as agreeing to fall in love." No more had to be said. She walked to the couch and lay down like any other patient.

Should one not consider that what went on during the few minutes while the patient was sitting in a chair facing me was analysis? She associated to what she had said and what she was doing—refusing to lie down and asking that she be allowed not to do so—in a meaningful way, I formed a conjecture—a very incomplete and preliminary one—about the nature of the underlying conflict and about the aspects of it that motivated her thought and behavior, I conveyed my conjecture to her as an interpretation, and a beneficial alteration resulted. It seems to me very hard to deny the name "analysis" to what went on while we were face to face.

But take another example. The patient referred to in Chapter 5 as an example of a "bad" patient remained in a chair face to face for a couple of years. The reader will recall that he had had a nearly catastrophic experience in "analysis" with a previous therapist, a man who represented himself as a really classical analyst trained in Europe in the 1930's. One proof of this "analyst's" self-proclaimed expertise had been his insistence that the patient use the couch. In that case the fact that the patient remained in a chair facing me for so very long, despite what I could understand and interpret to him of his unconscious reasons for doing so, was itself as good an indication as any of the miniscule rate of progress that was made in altering the psychic conflicts that were responsible for his extreme resistance to analysis. For all *practical* purposes, no analytic progress was possible while the patient sat up. Had he never been able to lie on the couch, I'd have to say he would never have made enough progress to dignify his treatment by calling it analysis. This is true, no doubt, because for such a patient his inability to use the couch is one of the consequences of the very conflicts that make any substantial degree of analytic progress impossible, but that does not change the practical importance of using the couch. Analysis is not possible if a patient does not use the couch, things being as they are in present-day analytic practice.

Nor is it possible to get around the difficulty by saying, "I don't even urge my patients to use the couch. They can do so or not as they wish. If they don't use the couch, it's no sign of resistance to analysis, so they can analyze just as well face to face as they can lying down."

The fact of the matter is that there are definite disadvantages to the face-to-face position and definite advantages to the recumbent one (see below). There is no good, practical reason for not instructing a patient to lie down so that he can enjoy the advantages thus available to him. It is true that as far as the history of psychoanalysis is concerned the couch is a relic of Freud's preanalytic, hypnotic technique. But it did not persist as an atavism. It is not anachronistic today. It is a useful part of the psychoanalytic situation. To fail to advise an analytic patient that it is to his advantage to use the couch is not technically desirable, therefore. At best it must raise questions in his mind about his analyst's reasons for having him remain in a chair and face to face — questions that complicate the transference unnecessarily and that must themselves be analyzed. At worst it obscures the patient's unconscious motives for avoiding the couch and contributes to rendering them and the conflicts of which they are part inaccessible to analysis.

If a patient is to be in analysis, it is to his advantage to use the couch and face away from his analyst. For him to do so substantially facilitates his saying freely whatever comes to his mind with as little interference as possible from external stimuli. When a patient is looking at his analyst he is necessarily influenced to some extent by his analyst's gestures, his position and movements, and his facial expression. To the extent that he is influenced in these ways, he is distracted from thoughts and feelings of his own that he would otherwise have been aware of. In a certain sense, therefore, for a patient to be in a position to watch his analyst is like introducing extraneous sights and sounds into one's office. Every analyst tries to have his office reasonably quiet and comfortably lighted so as not to distract his patients unnecessarily. Even this analogy is not a completely satisfactory one, however. It is, as has been said, true only in a certain sense, because in fact what his analyst may seem to a patient to convey by any sort of gesture is much more important and consequently much more influential and distracting in directing his thoughts and feelings than any other external sensory stimuli are likely to be. The transference of infantile wishes and conflicts onto the person of the analyst guarantees that this will be so. For this reason, then, it is of real, practical advantage for an analytic patient to use the couch. If he will not use it despite his analyst's suggestion that he do so, his inability or unwillingness is, essentially, a symptom of his psychic conflicts. Like any other symptom it is itself a clue to the nature of those conflicts and like other symptoms it should be analyzed in the usual way. Until it has been satisfactorily analyzed the patient will be face to face with his analyst as a matter of course, so one can say quite correctly that analysis can be carried on face to face under those circumstances. Should it be impossible to analyze the symptom, one would have to say that that patient wasn't analyzable. Treatable, maybe. Analyzable, no. In other words, one can do some analyzing face to face, but one cannot carry on an analysis in that way beyond a certain point. In that sense, then, one cannot analyze a patient face to face.

The situation is really quite analogous to that of an agoraphobic patient who must, at the start, be accompanied by a relative when he comes to his analyst's office. One neither forbids him to bring a companion nor ignores the fact that he must do so. One recognizes it as a symptom and proceeds to analyze it. If analysis is successful, the symptom disappears. If the symptom persists indefinitely, one knows that that patient has not "been analyzed"—that his analysis has not progressed satisfactorily—regardless of how much one thinks one has been able to understand of the nature and origins of the patient's conflicts. Analysis has failed. That patient has not been analyzed. No more can one be who is never able to "use the couch."

It is worth remembering, incidentally, that there is a whole class of analyses in which the couch is *not* used, namely, the analyses of children. Analysts are generally agreed that when one deals with a child below a certain age it is neither appropriate nor useful to use a couch. Other means must be sought to encourage a child to talk freely to his analyst. Here, then, is a major exception to the conclusion that analysis qua analysis means that a patient must be on the couch. Some analysts would account for the exception by saying that child analysis is something different from adult analysis, that it is only the name that is the same. They do not mean by this to deny the value of child analysis, either as therapy or as an investigative and research procedure, but only to say that child and adult analysis should not be equated because of the many differences between them with respect to technique, to transference, and to a child's whole life situation, in particular, his sexual development and capacities, both physical and psychological. Other analysts feel that the similarities are so much more important than the differences that the latter are merely incidental. Whichever of the two opinions one agrees with, and I myself favor the latter (Arlow and Brenner, 1966), the fact that the couch is not used in child analysis reminds us of a technical consideration that is vitally important even though it's so simple as to be obvious. The practical arrangements of analysis further the work of analysis only if they are acceptable to the patient. After all, their purpose is to help him talk and behave freely. If they're unconsciously too frightening, as in the illustrations given earlier, they're likely to make it harder for him to talk freely rather than easier. If they're incomprehensible and burdensomely restrictive, as lying for a whole session on a couch would be for a child, they'll have the same adverse effect. A patient's consent and cooperation are necessary with respect to all the practical arrangements, but it is just as necessary, if a patient objects to any reasonable and conventional practical arrangement, to discover why he does so. Insofar as his objections derive from his conflicts, it is important to deal with them analytically.

One of the implications of this general rule is that an analyst has to be clear in his own mind about which practical arrangements are important principally because they are essential to the analytic work, or at least helpful to it, and which ones are important and convenient to himself. This is not to say that the latter are less necessary or even less desirable than the former. It is to say only that the two should not be confused with one another.

For example, if an analyst stipulates that his patients pay him on the first of each month, he does so because it is convenient to him, for one reason or another, that they pay then. It has nothing to do with facilitating his patients' analyses. One can conduct an analysis just as well if one has his patients pay on any other day of the month, or, for that matter, on the first of each week, or if one makes no stipulation whatever, and merely hands the patient a bill on whatever day one chooses. Which arrangement is followed is rarely of any consequence to the progress of analysis. What is important is the meaning of the patient's reaction to whatever he is asked to do with regard to payment. Why does he object, remonstrate, fail to voice his objections, pay late, pay early, and so on? On this all analysts would agree. But in order to answer whichever of these questions applies to a particular patient one must start from the fact that whatever arrangement was made was the analyst's choice and is for his convenience. It won't do to tell a patient that it's "good" or "important" for his analysis that he pay on the first, the second, or whenever. It's not. As we have just said, any one of many different arrangements for paying fees is compatible with successful analysis. What's "good" for a patient's analysis is not that he pay on a particular day. That's something reasonable that he's being asked to do for practical reasons at his analyst's convenience. The patient has an obligation to do it as a reasonable adult, but not primarily because it is therapeutically advantageous to him as, for example, using the couch is. What's "good" for a patient's analysis as far as when and how he pays his fee is concerned is to analyze as thoroughly as possible what he thinks and feels about having to pay in conformity with his analyst's wishes or preference. What would be "bad" for analysis would be to fail to analyze those or any other thoughts and feelings that were important.

As a final illustrative example of practical arrangements, take the question of charging a patient for missed sessions. Freud (1913) advised that analysts charge for all missed sessions, but there are competent and experienced analysts who do not do so. Their arrangement is not to charge for a session that a patient missed for reasons beyond his control, e.g., because of a power failure in the subway, because of snow or ice that made roads impassable, or because of the death or serious illness of a close relative, and the like. Either arrangement is compatible with satisfactory analytic results, it seems, since there are some competent and experienced analysts who follow Freud's advice and others who do not. The question is whether either arrangement is likely to have an advantage over the other in some cases, at least.

After experimenting with both arrangements I have come to the conclusion that the one Freud advised is in fact preferable. Both from my own experience and from discussions with colleagues it seems to me that any other arrangement is too likely to be motivated by an analyst's unconscious desire to deny his own competitive and sadistic wishes. Where this is the case it is bound to lead to undesirable complications in the relation between analyst and patient. The objective fact is that the two are not on an equal footing. Patients come to analysts for many reasons, to be sure (see Nunberg, 1925), but in most cases one of the reasons is that they are sick and suffering. An analyst in his turn has many reasons for being an analyst and for accepting the patients he does accept for analysis, but one of his reasons in nearly every case is his pleasure in being a doctor. One cannot alter the fact that patients are sick and must agree to some extent to do what they're told if they want their analyst to help them get better, while an analyst profits from his patient's illness both in money and in personal satisfaction. It is obvious that these are not the only factors that determine the relationship that analyst and patient have with one another, but they are among the factors that do so. In some cases they are more important, in others, less so. Where they are important, they may not be ignored without impeding the work of analysis. The danger that this will happen is precisely what is involved in making an arrangement that presents an analyst as being careful to avoid an appearance of profiting from his patient's misfortune, i.e., as being free from any desire to do so. To say to a patient, "You need not pay if it was really your bad luck that kept you from keeping your appointment," is to present oneself in just such a light.

All in all, the most important thing to be kept in mind whenever one deals with the "practical arrangements" of analysis is this. Without exception they involve at least some elements of the transference, as was noted at the end of Chapter 1. How important those elements are, how usable they are analytically speaking, how accessible they are to conjecture and to interpretation will all vary from case to case and from instance to instance. But they cannot fail to be present from the very nature of the situation, which is that the analyst does something or proposes to do something to which the patient is asked to conform. Some of the determinants of any patient's reaction in such a situation must derive from his infantile instinctual conflicts. This will be true whether the arrangement is primarily advantageous analytically or primarily a matter of convenience, either mutual or one-sided. It cannot be otherwise and an analyst should always take the fact that it cannot into consideration both in the way he makes his practical arrangements and in the attention he pays to his patients' reactions to them. Like symptoms, they are too apt to be undervalued or even overlooked as useful clues to the nature and origin of a patient's psychic conflicts.

Let us turn now from the subject of the practical

arrangements that are a part of every analytic situation to a subject of an even more general nature, that of free association.

"Free association" is one of the most familiar terms in the vocabulary of psychoanalysis. Not infrequently it's used to define the psychoanalytic method: "Psychoanalysis is the technique, or the method, of free association." We're sometimes told that a good analytic patient is a patient with an aptitude for free association. We also hear just the opposite, namely, that it is rare for a patient to "really" free associate, or even that when a patient *can* really free associate, it's a sign that he's thoroughly analyzed, that his analysis is over.

All such statements refer to clinical data that are both familiar and important. It is the fact that they're expressed in terms of "free association" that makes them confusing or even mutually contradictory. "Free association" is a bad term to apply to the psychoanalytic method. It is bad for two reasons. First, because it obscures the fact that an analytic patient is often asked to associate to a specific conscious stimulus. And, second, and more important, because it obscures the fact that Freud's great discovery, the discovery that became the very cornerstone of psychoanalytic technique, was that associations are never "free." They are, on the contrary, always caused by some psychic stimuli or other.

As to the first reason, every analyst knows that during the course of an analysis he often has occasion to direct his patient's attention to one thing or another with the suggestion, however it may be conveyed, that it is worthwhile to think about. Asking a patient to think about something, whether the "something" is a dream, a symptom, a parapraxis, a daydream, a physical sensation, a metaphor, an occurrence of the day before or one of his early childhood, is so common and so integral a part of analytic technique that it requires no careful description. The use of the term "free association" as a synonym for the psychoanalytic method thus has the disadvantage of seeming to suggest that it is not good analytic technique to "direct" a patient's associations in any way, something that is far from the truth.

As to the second reason, we all know that what Freud discovered, and what every subsequent analyst has abundantly confirmed is that, to the extent that anyone renounces conscious control over his thoughts, to the degree that he ignores his customary conscious interests, unconscious stimuli take over and control his thoughts. Instead of his thoughts being "associations" to ideas he knows of, they are associations to unconscious ideas, fantasies, wishes, etc. Nothing could be more familiar or more elementary. The ambiguity and the inconsistencies arise from the fact that we know today much more of the particulars of mental functioning than was known in the very early years of the development of psychoanalysis. When first introduced, "free association" meant to psychoanalysts "free of the repressive and distorting influences of the conscious mind." If only those influences could be set aside, psychoanalysis thought, if only a patient could suspend them temporarily, his unconscious, infantile wishes and memories would pour forth without distortion or hindrance, freed from the barrier of repression. It is this idea that accounts for the colloquial usages of the terms "free association" and "to free associate" with which we are all familiar. They were terms that served the needs of analysts only as long as their knowledge of mental functioning was in its early stages. They do so no longer. Nothing that anyone thinks or says is ever free from repression and other defenses. Every thought, every "association" is necessarily a compromise formation among the various tendencies of the mind, tendencies that we call forces and that we group under the headings of id, ego, and superego. We no longer expect or hope a patient to put his defenses and his superego out of commission even temporarily so that his id derivatives will emerge unhindered. What we do hope to accomplish is something that we understand quite differently, something to which the term "free association" does not seem appropriate in anything like its old sense. We create a situation, both physically and psychologically, that will keep extraneous and incidental stimuli to a minimum and we encourage patients to communicate their thoughts without editing them. Largely from what a patient then tells us we form a conjecture concerning the nature and origin of his psychic conflicts and of their relation to his current mental functioning: his feelings, thoughts, dreams, fantasies, symptoms, and so on. By means of interpretations based on our conjectures we alter the patient's conflicts so that, among other things, he can tolerate less distorted derivatives of his infantile instinctual wishes. As a result of all this the patient becomes freer if you will. Freer of anxiety, of guilt, and of depressive affects, and, we hope, freer of symptoms, inhibitions, and suffering. The word "free" is aptly descriptive of the changes that occur when it is used in that sense. But a patient's thoughts, his associations, are never free of the influence of ego and superego functioning. It's not possible for them to be, as far as we know. They are always compromise formations, as much so at the end of a successful analysis as they were at the beginning. We can go even farther, in fact, and say that, true as it is that associations are never free in the old sense of the word, not even at the end of a good analysis, it is just as true that every association, even at the beginning of the most difficult, least successful analysis is in part an expression of an infantile instinctual wish, since it is necessarily a compromise in the formation of which id derivatives play their part.

The fact that a psychoanalyst does not expect any patient's defenses ever to disappear also affects his attitude as he listens to his patient's productions. He knows that all that is possible is a shift in the balance of forces within the mind, an alteration in a patient's psychic conflict that has as a consequence the appearance of less disguised derivatives of the patient's instinctual wishes in his conscious thoughts and, consequently, in what he says — in his associations — as he lies on the couch. What an analyst hears from a patient is invariably a compromise formation that results from his instinctual derivatives, the pleasurable and unpleasurable affects associated with them, the defenses and related reactions triggered by anxiety and depressive affects, and the influence of current circumstances or events. An analyst's attention may be directed, quite properly, to one or another of this welter of determinants as he listens to a patient. Not all are equally important at any given moment to the task of enlarging his understanding of the patient — conjecture formation — and of conveying his understanding to the patient — interpretation. He knows that all are there in the analytic material, nevertheless, and that each will engage his attention at some later time as it has in the past. It is this distribution of interest among the several components of the mental apparatus that Anna Freud

(1936) described so eloquently in the initial pages of her classic monograph. An analyst cannot work otherwise if he is to apply what he knows about the mind — psychoanalytic theory — to what he does in his daily work — psychoanalytic practice. In his day-to-day work he must perceive in each patient's associations the constant interaction of the forces that he knows are responsible for them. His perception of those forces may be conscious or unconscious, intuitive, inferred, or reasoned, as was noted in Chapter 2, but he must perceive them in one way or another if his clinical practice is to profit fully from his theoretical knowledge, i.e., from the distillate of his own experience and that of his colleagues.

There was a time when psychoanalytic theory was mainly concerned with psychopathology. It is true that in retrospect one can see that it was never only a theory of psychopathology. One can discern in it from its very beginnings the germs of many of the ideas that are applied today to the understanding of normal aspects of mental functioning as well. At the time, however, such an application evoked little interest. Psychopathology was the main concern of psychoanalysis and patients were divided into two parts, as it were, one normal and the other pathological. The latter was an analyst's proper concern. With the former he need have little to do in practice.

In more recent years analysts have had an increasing appreciation of the fact that the normal and the pathological in mental life are so closely linked together as to form what is essentially a coherent whole. Patients are no longer to be divided into separate parts. Each patient is an indivisible, coherent whole and must be studied and understood as a whole. As a result analysis has become both a more extensive and a more profound venture than was formerly the case. It has become nothing less than an attempt to understand, from *all* of their consequences in his mental life, the nature and origins of a person's most important psychic conflicts.

The greater usefulness of such a holistic approach must be apparent. It affords an analyst a more unified and a more integrated understanding of his patients than would be possible otherwise. For instance, in the case of the patient whose fear of flying recurred after it had been absent for many months (see Chapter 6), one can see how closely related were her phobia and certain aspects of her work. Both were intimately connected with her penis envy and her childhood incestuous wishes and each threw a different, one might say a complementary light upon them. Analyzing her symptom helped to demonstrate that one of her childhood wishes was to bite off someone's penis — her brother's, her father's, or both — and thus become herself a man instead of "just a girl." At the same time her relations with her superior and her peers at work added two additional bits of information, one, that one of her reasons for so desiring to have a penis and be a boy was her conviction that if she were a boy her father would love her best, and the other, that her hatred of men sprang partly from her anger at her father for not having loved her best when she was a child. When her superior did promote her, she ate the sausages and promptly fell ill, just as she had while performing fellatio on her boyfriend. Symptom, vocational success, relationships with fellow workers, sexual life, and dietary preference are all interrelated via their connections with the patient's infantile instinctual conflicts. One learns most about those conflicts by putting together their normal and their pathological consequences. By doing so an analyst learns much more than he can by considering either set of consequences separately, or any single consequence, whether normal or pathological, in isolation from all the others. The patient herself told of her anxiety and nausea. She spontaneously added the memory of her sexual experience. She did not, however, add the fact that the trip followed on her promotion and was a sign of her success,· so to speak, nor did she refer explicitly to her feelings about her superior. Those facts, though consciously familiar to her, were isolated at the time she told of the recurrence of her neurotic symptom and their connection with its recurrence had to be interpreted to her.

In this example the connections were easy to make. The analytic material on which they were based was neither very extensive nor specially obscure. In other instances the difficulties in the way of connecting and correlating superficially disparate material are much greater. The material is more voluminous, the connections are more hidden, the common factors are less familiar and hence less easy to discover. But whether it be easy or difficult, whether it be immediately soluble or eventually impossible, there will always be an advantage to approaching a patient's mental life as a whole rather than as a conglomerate of fragments that are only loosely held together. An analyst can accomplish the task of understanding a patient's conflicts most easily, most thoroughly, and most expeditiously if it is second nature for him to see the patient as a whole person and not as two persons, the one sick and the other well. Whatever a patient does or says, however "normal" it may be, is informative about his conflicts to a greater or lesser degree. Human thought and behavior *are* conflict, as Kris (1947) observed long ago.

A holistic approach, then, based as it is on that part of psychoanalytic theory that concerns the relation between psychic conflict and conscious thought and behavior, is valuable as part of an analyst's orientation to people in general and to patients in particular. It's not something to be applied in a particular situation, something one finds useful only under special circumstances. It is, on the contrary, fundamental to one's whole attitude. It is part of one's knowledge of how people are.

Another similar bit of knowledge is also helpful as a part of one's orientation in analytic practice. It is true of every adult, and conspicuously so for analytic patients, that the child he once was lives on within him. Of the many meanings that can be given to this cliché, the one that is important here has to do with the fact that psychic conflicts originate from the instinctual wishes of infancy and that they are largely shaped into a lasting form during those years. The psychic conflicts of adult life are childish in the literal sense of the word. Unknown to the patient, at least at the beginning of analysis, the child he once was still lives within him, with all the passions, the fears, the misery, the defenses that the words "psychic conflict" denote. It is true that the childish nucleus is disguised, distorted, and more or less heavily overlaid by the psychic accretions of later years, but it is also true that analysis tries to reverse the process of accretion, to roll back the subsequent alterations and to reveal as fully as possible the little child that once was and still is, despite all the changes that have taken place.

One often sees the child in action with special clarity in the transference. Perhaps this is because of the nature of transference itself, perhaps it is because the analytic situation so often tends to make the transference the principal focus of the patient's wishes and hence of the analyst's attention. Whatever the reason, the result is there. In the transference one is dealing at bottom with a small child and the knowledge that this is the case is often helpful. When a patient behaves toward his analyst in a way that is childishly demanding, childishly complaining, childishly unreasonable, childishly fantastic, or childishly anything else — angry, stubborn, tearful, or what not — one should be neither surprised nor critical. How else can one expect a child to behave? That's the way children are, as one discovers from having analyzed enough adults, paradoxical as it sounds to say so.

The practical value of recognizing the child in an adult patient's transference reaction became apparent to me first in connection with some instances of negative therapeutic reaction (Brenner, 1959). I know of no other explicit reference to the matter in the psychoanalytic literature, certainly not in the literature on psychoanalytic technique. Yet I doubt very much that my recommendation in this regard is in any way an original one. Both the observations on which it is based and the understanding of those observations are too familiar for that to be the case. The idea that the child that was lives on in the man that is was a cliché long before psychoanalysis was ever thought of. What seemed to me valuable in 1959 was to put new meaning into this timeworn cliché by adding to it the more profound significance that psychoanalysis has brought to it and to apply it, thus enriched and expanded, in dealing with a special problem of psychoanalytic technique. I may add that in the intervening years I have been repeatedly impressed by the fact that it is valuable as part of an analyst's attitude toward all his patients all the time.

SUMMARY

1. The goal of psychoanalysis in general is best defined as the maximum beneficial alteration of a patient's psychic conflicts that can be achieved by analytic means.

2. In individual cases analytic goals are limited. Psychic conflicts can never disappear. They can only change so that the resulting compromise formations are clinically normal rather than clinically pathological.

3. Such changes must not be thought to be of only minor consequence. On the contrary, they are often of very great importance and value to a patient. Their importance is all the greater because, when analysis is successful, its beneficial results are always widespread.

4. A patient's apparent lack of progress in analysis can be due to one or more than one of several causes. Only analytic scrutiny can help decide which is important in a particular case.

5. An assessment of the degree to which it is possible by analytic means to achieve a beneficial alteration of a patient's psychic conflicts plays a role in two aspects of analytic practice that seem at first glance to be unrelated, even antithetical, namely, in case selection and in termination.

6. In selecting cases for analysis one tries to decide, on the basis of data that are necessarily limited and often inadequate, how likely it is that one can understand and beneficially alter a patient's conflicts to a sufficient extent to justify the time, the effort, and the expense of analysis.

7. In deciding when to terminate an analysis one

tries to decide, on the basis of data that are much more plentiful and that one hopes are fully adequate in successful cases at least, whether the prospects for further beneficial alteration of a patient's conflict speak in favor of interrupting or terminating analysis in the not too distant future.

8. So-called forced termination is of doubtful value in analysis.

9. So-called practical arrangements in analysis necessarily involve and are involved in the transference. They must be understood in this light and, when necessary, the patient's reaction to them should be analyzed as a manifestation or part of the transference. To illustrate and document this, use of the couch, schedule of payment, and responsibility for missed sessions are discussed. Reference is also made to features of child-analytic technique that illuminate certain aspects of psychoanalytic technique with adult patients.

10. "Free association" is an undesirable term to apply to the psychoanalytic method for two reasons:

a. Because patients in analysis often associate to designated, consciously perceived stimuli such as dreams, symptoms, etc.

b. Because the cornerstone of the psychoanalytic method, i.e., of psychoanalytic technique, is that a patient's associations are never "free." To the degree that a patient renounces conscious control over his thoughts they are determined by unconscious stimuli — by the unconscious influences that are active in his mind.

11. If his analysis is successful, a patient becomes freer — freer of anxiety, guilt, and depressive affects, of symptoms, inhibitions, and suffering — but his associations are always compromise formations. They are never

free of defenses, never free of the restrictive and distorting influences of ego and superego functioning. At the end of analysis, as at its beginning, associations are compromises among id, ego, and superego.

12. Psychic conflicts result in normal compromise formations as well as pathological ones. It is, therefore, useful to have a holistic approach, one that includes an interest in both normal and pathological compromise formations and that attempts to relate all of them to one another to the extent that such a relationship exists.

13. The adage that the child lives on in the man, or adult, can be useful as a guideline to the best solution of many technical problems in psychoanalysis.

8

CONCLUSION

A book like this one, devoted to exposition, is usually a monologue. Yet in writing it I felt that if it is to serve its purpose well, what appears on its pages as a monologue must be the result of a dialogue, at least in my mind, between myself and my intended audience — an audience consisting of colleagues who are already practicing psychoanalysis or who intend to practice it. As I was writing I kept asking my colleagues — in my imagination — whether what I had to say was something they knew already and had no interest in rereading or whether they found it fresh and novel enough to spend some time on. In each instance I was guided toward reaching a decision by what I supposed their answer would be. In effect I followed their instructions. The result is a book that is much shorter than it would otherwise have been. I hope that it is also more stimulating and more thought-provoking than it would be if I had been less attentive to what I imagined my intended readers' wishes to be.

I have tried throughout the book to make it a useful supplement to its readers' experience. As I said in the introduction, I believe that no book on technique can be more than such a supplement. One cannot learn analysis except by doing it. Experience is no less necessary than is understanding to the development of a skillful technique. The best technician will combine the two. Experience illuminated by understanding is the ideal toward which every psychoanalyst strives.

My professional life has been devoted primarily to the practice of psychoanalysis. During the course of it, as one would expect, I have had my share of dramatic and unusual clinical experiences, but I have been careful not to include any of them here. Such experiences have the advantage, when they are used as illustrations, of riveting the attention and interest of the reader. But they have drawbacks as well, not the least of which is the possibility that they may give the reader the impression that they are the rule rather than the exception in one's practice. On balance it has seemed to me to be preferable to avoid them for the purposes that I hope this book will serve. Consequently the illustrative examples that have been chosen are all commonplace, everyday ones. They are run of the mine examples, not gem specimens. They illustrate the day-to-day stuff of analysis. It is in such stuff that its greatest fascination seems to me to lie. It is there that one finds the most formidable challenges to an analyst's understanding and to his technical proficiency. If he can understand the complex determinants of everyday analytic material, if he can maintain an analytic attitude day in and day out, if he can convey his conjectures— understanding—successfully in the form of interpretations as the days and weeks go by, he need have no fear of his ability to understand the rare, the dramatic, and the bizarre, and to deal with it analytically when it comes his way.

For many who practice analysis its chief fascination lies in its value as a form of psychotherapy. That this is an essential component of the personal reward from analysis for everyone who practices it seems almost certain. It is hard to imagine anyone spending his life as an analyst unless the role of therapist is an important source of gratification for him. It follows that for every analyst there is a pleasure that comes from broadening his experience and improving his technical proficiency. Whether consciously or not, he surely hopes that each analytic task well done is at the same time the means or the basis for doing the next one better and more easily or, if not that, for anticipating more knowledgeably the unavoidable difficulties and delays. Should this book enable its readers to profit more from their clinical experience by suggesting to them new and useful ways of approaching some of the technical problems they face, it will have accomplished its principal purpose. But perhaps it will do more. Perhaps it will also assist some in exploiting the potential that I believe psychoanalytic practice has for the exploration of the human mind and for new discoveries about it. Bush (1945) called the whole of science an endless frontier and I for one see no end as yet to what remains to be learned by the application of the psychoanalytic method. Since this is a point on which not all analysts agree, a few words of discussion are in order.

Every writer on psychoanalytic technique is agreed on its fruitfulness in the past as a method of investigation. This agreement has entered into the very definition of the word "psychoanalysis," a definition that was given succinctly by Hartmann and Kris (1945) as threefold: a therapeutic technique, an investigative (or, to use their word, "observational") method, and a body of hypotheses. By developing and applying the psychoanalytic method Freud, in a single lifetime, learned more about human psychology than has been discovered since the dawn of science, two thousand years ago, by all other means together. But in recent years doubts have been raised by some analysts as to whether the psychoanalytic method is likely to lead to any important new discoveries and whether, in addition, it meets the criteria that should properly be set for any scientific method (Kubie, 1975, p. 325; Gill et al., 1968; Wallerstein and Sampson, 1971; Fisher, personal communication, 1975). Whatever the differences among these many authors, they are united in maintaining that, as a method of scientific prospecting, the practice of analysis—the use of its technique in a merely therapeutic setting, devoid of tape recorders, computers, and the like—is played out. In their view all the nuggets have been gathered by now—mostly by Freud and his nearest followers chronologically—and more subtle or more systematic means than those of clinical observation are needed to refine the ore that remains and to extract from it new facts and new hypotheses. The consulting room as it stands, they say, is no longer a fruitful laboratorium, however valuable it may be therapeutically or even educationally, for no worker in the field who has himself been analyzed denies or underrates the value of analysis as part of training for both therapy and research. But the period of naturalistic observation is over in the history of psychoanalysis, we are told, and a new period must begin in which other scientific methods are used.

These prophets may be right. Whether right or

wrong—for who can prophesy with certainty in any field of science?—they should certainly be encouraged and supported in their own researches, whatever the methods they use. Every approach that has reason in it is worth following as energetically and as enthusiastically as possible. My reason for having introduced the subject is to disagree only to the extent that psychoanalytic technique is derogated with respect to its usefulness as a method of research in the current scene. I believe that it is still useful and that much remains to be discovered by applying it skillfully and persistently. I believe that psychoanalysis is a branch of science that for a long time to come will offer much in the way of the satisfaction of a desire to learn more and to discover what has been previously unknown. Whoever has a desire to engage in such explorations will find means to gratify it in pursuing his therapeutic work as an analyst.

REFERENCES

Alexander, F. (1930), *Psychoanalysis of the Total Personality*. New York & Washington: Nervous & Mental Disease Publishing Co.

———— (1933), The relation of structural and instinctual conflicts. *Psychoanal. Quart.*, 2:181-207.

Arlow, J. A. (1969a), Unconscious fantasy and disturbances of conscious experience. *Psychoanal. Quart.*, 38:1-27.

———— (1969b), Fantasy, memory and reality testing. *Psychoanal. Quart.*, 38:28-51.

———— & Brenner, C. (1964), *Psychoanalytic Concepts and the Structural Theory*. New York: International Universities Press.

———— ———— (1966), The psychoanalytic situation. In: *Psychoanalysis in the Americas,* ed. R. E. Littman. New York: International Universities Press, pp. 23-43.

Atkins, N. B. (1968), Acting out and psychosomatic illness as related regressive trends. *Internat. J. Psycho-Anal.*, 49:221-223.

Balint, M. (1961), Contribution to discussion at the 22nd International Psycho-Analytical Congress. Unpublished.

Baranger, M. & Baranger, W. (1966), Insight in the analytic situation. In: *Psychoanalysis in the Americas,* ed. R. E. Littman. New York: International Universities Press, pp. 56-72.

Beres, D. (1956), Ego deviation and the concept of schizophrenia. *The Psychoanalytic Study of the Child,* 11:164-235. New York: International Universities Press.

———— (1966), Superego and depression. In: *Psychoanalysis—A General Psychology,* ed. R. M. Loewenstein et al. New York: International Universities Press, pp. 479-498.

———— & Arlow, J. A. (1974), Fantasy and identification in empathy. *Psychoanal. Quart.*, 43:26-50.

Bonaparte, M. (1945), Notes on the analytic discovery of a primal scene. *The Psychoanalytic Study of the Child,* 1:119-125. New York: International Universities Press.

Brenner, C. (1953), An addendum to Freud's theory of anxiety. *Internat. J. Psycho-Anal.*, 34:18-24.

———— (1955), *An Elementary Textbook of Psychoanalysis* [1st ed.]. New York: International Universities Press.

———— (1959), The masochistic character, genesis and treatment. *J. Amer. Psychoanal. Assn.,* 7 197-226.

———— (1966), The mechanism of repression. In: *Psychoanalysis—A General Psychology,* ed. R. M. Loewenstein et al. New York: International Universities Press, pp. 390-399.

———— (1968a), Archaic features of ego functioning. *Internat. J. Psycho-Anal.,* 49:426-430.

———— (1968b), Psychoanalysis and science. *J. Amer. Psychoanal. Assn.,* 16:675-696.

———— (1969a), Metapsychology and neurophysiology. Discussion of paper by R. W. Gardner. *J. Amer. Psychoanal. Assn.,* 17:41-53.

———— (1969b), Some comments on technical precepts in psychoanalysis. *J. Amer. Psychoanal. Assn.,* 17:333-352.

———— (1970), Psychoanalysis: philosophy or science? In: *Psychoanalysis and Philosophy,* ed. C. Hanly & M. Lazerowitz. New York: International Universities Press, pp. 35-45.

———— (1971), The psychoanalytic concept of aggression. *Internat. J. Psycho-Anal.,* 52:137-144.

———— (1973a), *An Elementary Textbook of Psychoanalysis,* 2nd ed. New York: International Universities Press.

———— (1973b), Theory and therapy in psychoanalysis. In: *Papers in Honor of Richard Sterba,* ed. A. Grinstein. Unpublished.

———— (1974a), Some observations on depression, on nosology, on affects and on mourning. *J. Geriat. Psychiat.,* 7:6-20.

———— (1974b), On the nature and development of affects: a unified theory. *Psychoanal. Quart.,* 43:532-556.

———— (1975a), Affects and psychic conflict. *Psychoanal. Quart.,* 44:5-28.

———— (1975b), Alterations in defenses during psychoanalysis. In: *Monographs of the Kris Study Group of the New York Psychoanalytic Institute,* 6:1-22, ed. H. F. Waldhorn & B. D. Fine. New York: International Universities Press.

Brunswick, R. M. (1928), A supplement to Freud's *History of an Infantile Neurosis. Internat. J. Psycho-Anal.,* 9:439-476.

Bush, V. (1945), *Science: The Endless Frontier.* Washington, D.C.: U.S. Government Printing Office.

Demaria, L. A. de (1968), Homosexual acting out. *Internat. J. Psycho-Anal.,* 49:219-220.

De Mijolla, A. & Shentoub, S. A. (1973), *Pour une Psychanalyse de l'Alcoholisme.* Paris: Payot.

Fenichel, O. (1941), *Problems of Psychoanalytic Technique*. Albany, N.Y.: The Psychoanalytic Quarterly.

———— (1945), Neurotic acting out. In: *The Collected Papers of Otto Fenichel*, 2:296-304. New York: Norton, 1954.

Fischer, C. (1975), personal communication.

Freud, A. (1936), *The Ego and the Mechanisms of Defense. The Writings of Anna Freud*, Vol. 2. New York: International Universities Press, 1966.

———— (1968), Acting out. *Internat. J. Psycho-Anal.*, 49:165-170.

Freud, S. (1899), Screen memories. *Standard Edition*, 3:301-322. London: Hogarth Press, 1962.

———— (1900), The interpretation of dreams. *Standard Edition*, 4 & 5. London: Hogarth Press, 1953.

———— (1904), Freud's psycho-analytic procedure. *Standard Edition*, 7:247-254. London: Hogarth Press, 1953.

———— (1905), Fragment of an analysis of a case of hysteria. *Standard Edition*, 7:1-122. London: Hogarth Press, 1953.

———— (1908), Hysterical phantasies and their relation to bisexuality. *Standard Edition*, 9:155-166. London: Hogarth Press, 1959.

———— (1910), The future prospects of psycho-analytic therapy. *Standard Edition*, 11:141-151. London: Hogarth Press, 1957.

———— (1911), Psycho-analytic notes on an autobiographical account of a case of paranoia (dementia paranoides). *Standard Edition*, 12:1-82. London: Hogarth Press, 1958.

———— (1912a), The dynamics of transference. *Standard Edition*, 12:97-108. London: Hogarth Press, 1958.

———— (1912b), Recommendations to physicians practising psychoanalysis. *Standard Edition*, 12:109-120. London: Hogarth Press, 1958.

———— (1913), On beginning the treatment. *Standard Edition*, 12:121-144. London: Hogarth Press, 1958.

———— (1914), Remembering, repeating and working-through. *Standard Edition*, 12:145-156. London: Hogarth Press, 1958.

———— (1915), Observations on transference-love. *Standard Edition*, 12:157-171. London: Hogarth Press, 1958.

———— (1916), Some character types met with in psycho-analytic work. *Standard Edition*, 14:309-335. London: Hogarth Press, 1957.

———— (1917a), Mourning and melancholia. *Standard Edition*, 14:237-258. London: Hogarth Press, 1957.

———— (1917b), Introductory lectures on psycho-analysis. *Standard Edition*, 15 & 16. London: Hogarth Press, 1963.

———— (1918), From the history of an infantile neurosis. *Standard Edition*, 17:1-122. London: Hogarth Press, 1955.

———— (1919), A child is being beaten. *Standard Edition*, 17:175-204. London: Hogarth Press, 1955.

———— (1920), Beyond the pleasure principle. *Standard Edition*, 18:1-64. London: Hogarth Press, 1955.

———— (1923a), The ego and the id. *Standard Edition*, 19:1-59. London: Hogarth Press, 1961.

———— (1923b), Remarks on the theory and practice of dream interpretation. *Standard Edition*, 19:109-122. London: Hogarth Press, 1961.

———— (1924), The economic problem of masochism. *Standard Edition*, 19:155-170. London: Hogarth Press, 1961.

———— (1926), Inhibitions, symptoms and anxiety. *Standard Edition*, 20:75-172. London: Hogarth Press, 1959.

———— (1933), New introductory lectures on psycho-analysis. *Standard Edition*, 22:1-182. London: Hogarth Press, 1964.

———— (1937), Constructions in analysis. *Standard Edition*, 23:255-270. London: Hogarth Press, 1964.

Garbarino, H. (1968), Contribution to symposium on acting out. *Internat. J. Psycho-Anal.*, 49:193-194.

Gill, M. M., et al. (1968), Studies in audio-recorded psychoanalysis. *J. Amer. Psychoanal. Assn.*, 16:230-244.

Greenacre, P. (1953), Penis awe and its relation to penis envy. In: *Drives, Affects and Behavior*, ed. R. M. Loewenstein. New York: International Universities Press, pp. 176-190.

———— (1968), The psychoanalytic process, transference, and acting out. *Internat. J. Psycho-Anal.*, 49:211-218.

Greenson, R. R. (1958), Variations in classical psychoanalytic technique: an introduction. *Internat. J. Psycho-Anal.*, 39:200-201.

———— (1967), *The Technique and Practice of Psychoanalysis*. New York: International Universities Press.

———— (1974), Loving, hating and indifference toward the patient. *Internat. Rev. Psycho-Anal.*, 1:259-266.

Grinberg, L. (1968), On acting out and its role in the psycho-analytic process. *Internat. J. Psycho-Anal.*, 49:171-178.

Hartmann, H. & Kris, E. (1945), The genetic approach in psychoanalysis. *The Psychoanalytic Study of the Child,* 1:11-30. New York: International Universities Press.

———————— & Loewenstein, R. M. (1949), Notes on the theory of aggression. *The Psychoanalytic Study of the Child,* 3/4:9-36. New York: International Universities Press.

Heimann, P. (1950), On counter-transference. *Internat. J. Psycho-Anal.,* 31:81-84.

Hermann, I. (1933), *Die Psychoanalyse als Methode.* Vienna: Internationaler Psychoanalytischer Verlag, 1934.

Hoffer, W. (1954), Defensive process and defensive organization: their place in psycho-analytic technique. *Internat. J. Psycho-Anal.,* 35:194-198.

Isaacs, S. (1939), Criteria for interpretation. *Internat. J. Psycho-Anal.,* 20:148-160.

Klein, M. (1935), A contribution to the psychogenesis of manic-depressive states. *Internat. J. Psycho-Anal.,* 16:145-174.

Kohut, H. (1959), Introspection, empathy and psychoanalysis. An examination of the relationship between mode of observation and theory. *J. Amer. Psychoanal. Assn.,* 7:459-483.

Kris, E. (1947), The nature of psychoanalytic propositions and their validation. In: *Freedom and Experience,* ed. S. Hook & M. R. Konwitz. Ithaca, N.Y.: Cornell University Press, pp. 239-259.

——— (1951), Ego psychology and interpretation in psychoanalytic therapy. *Psychoanal. Quart.,* 20:15-30.

——— (1956), The recovery of childhood memories in psychoanalysis. *The Psychoanalytic Study of the Child,* 11:54-88. New York: International Universities Press.

Kubie, L. S. (1952), Problems and techniques of psychoanalytic validation and progress. In: *Psychoanalysis as Science,* ed. E. Pumpian-Mindlin. Stanford, Calif.: Stanford University Press, pp. 46-124.

——— (1975), *Practical and Theoretical Aspects of Psychoanalysis,* rev. ed. New York: International Universities Press.

Lebovici, S. (1968), Contribution to the symposium on acting out. *Internat. J. Psycho-Anal.,* 49:202-205.

Levin, A. J. (1957), Œdipus and Samson. The rejected hero child. *Internat. J. Psycho-Anal.,* 38:105-116.

Lewin, B. D. (1952), Phobic symptoms and dream interpretation. *Psychoanal. Quart.,* 21:295-322.

Little, M. (1951), Counter-transference and the patient's response to it. *Internat. J. Psycho-Anal.*, 32:32-40.

Loewenstein, R. M. (1954), Some remarks on defences, autonomous ego, and psychoanalytic technique. *Internat. J. Psycho-Anal.*, 35:188-193.

Malcove, L. (1975), The analytic situation: toward a view of the supervisory experience. *J. Philadelphia Assn. Psychoanal.*, 2:1-14.

Mitscherlich-Nielsen, M. (1968), Contribution to the symposium on acting out. *Internat. J. Psycho-Anal.*, 49:188-192.

Money-Kyrle, R. E. (1956), Normal counter-transference and some of its deviations. *Internat. J. Psycho-Anal.*, 37:360-366.

Moore, B. E. (1968), Contribution to the symposium on acting out. *Internat. J. Psycho-Anal.*, 49:182-184.

Nunberg, H. (1925), The will to recovery. *Internat. J. Psycho-Anal.*, 7:64-78, 1926.

Panel (1954), Defense mechanisms and psychoanalytic technique, rep. E. R. Zetzel. *J. Amer. Psychoanal. Assn.*, 2:318-326.

———— (1955), Validation of psychoanalytic techniques, rep. J. Marmor. *J. Amer. Psychoanal. Assn.*, 3:496-505.

———— (1967), Defense organization of the ego and psychoanalytic technique, rep. E. Pumpian-Mindlin. *J. Amer. Psychoanal. Assn.*, 15:150-165.

———— (1970), The fate of the defenses in the psychoanalytic process, rep. J. Krent. *J. Amer. Psychoanal. Assn.*, 18:177-194.

———— (1972), Continuing research: the modification of defenses in psychoanalysis, rep. J. Weiss. *J. Amer. Psychoanal. Assn.*, 20: 177-198.

Rado, S. (1933), Fear of castration in women. *Psychoanal. Quart.*, 2:425-475.

Rangell, L. (1968), A point of view on acting out. *Internat. J. Psycho-Anal.*, 49:195-201.

Rascovsky, A. & Rascovsky, M. (1968), On the genesis of acting out and psychopathic behavior in Sophocles' *Œdipus*. *Internat. J. Psycho-Anal.*, 49:390-394.

Reich, A. (1951), On counter-transference. *Internat. J. Psycho-Anal.*, 32:25-31.

Reidy, J. J. (1975), Contribution to discussion at meeting of Baltimore-D.C. Psychoanalytic Society, 22 March.

Reik, T. (1937), *Surprise and the Psychoanalyst.* New York: Dutton.

Report (1968), Reports of discussions of acting out. *Internat. J. Psycho-Anal.,* 49:224-230.

——— (1969), Superego analysis. Report by members of the Ernst Kris Study Group of the New York Psychoanalytic Institute. Abst. in *Psychoanal. Quart.,* 40:189-190.

Riviere, J. (1936), On the genesis of psychical conflict in earliest infancy. *Internat. J. Psycho-Anal.,* 17:395-422.

Rosen, V. H. (1955), The reconstruction of a traumatic childhood event in a case of derealization. *J. Amer. Psychoanal. Assn.,* 3:211-221.

Rouart, J. (1968), Acting out and the psychoanalytic process. *Internat. J. Psycho-Anal.,* 49:185-187.

Sandler, J., et al. (1970), Basic psychoanalytic concepts: II. The treatment alliance. *Brit. J. Psychiat.,* 116:555-558.

Saussure, R. de (1954), Mechanisms of defence and their place in psycho-analytic therapy. *Internat. J. Psycho-Anal.,* 35:199-201.

Schmideberg, M. (1949), "Error" and "proof" in analytic conclusions. *Samiksa,* 3:254-261.

Schmidl, F. (1955), The problem of scientific validation in psychoanalytic interpretations. *Internat. J. Psycho-Anal.,* 36:105-113.

Schwarz, H. (1968), Contribution to the symposium on acting out. *Internat. J. Psycho-Anal.,* 49:179-181.

Stein, M. H. (1953), Premonition as a defense. *Psychoanal. Quart.,* 22:69-74.

Strachey, J. (1934), The nature of the therapeutic action of psychoanalysis. *Internat. J. Psycho-Anal.,* 15:127-159. (Reprinted in the same journal, 50:275-292, 1969).

Ticho, E. A. (1972), Termination of psychoanalysis: treatment goals, life goals. *Psychoanal. Quart.,* 41:315-333.

Tyson, R. L. & Sandler, J. (1971), Problems in the selection of patients for psychoanalysis: comments on the application of the concepts of 'indications,' 'suitability' and 'analyzability.' *Brit. J. Med. Psychol.,* 44:211-228.

Vanggaard, T. (1968), Contribution to the symposium on acting out. *Internat. J. Psycho-Anal.,* 49:206-210.

Waelder, R. (1930), The principle of multiple function. *Psychoanalysis: Observation, Theory, Application.* New York: International Universities Press, 1976, pp. 68-83.

——— (1939), Criteria of interpretation. *Psychoanalysis: Observation, Theory, Application.* New York: International Universities Press, 1976, pp. 189-199.

——— (1956), Introduction to the discussion on problems of transference. *Psychoanalysis: Observation, Theory, Application.* New York: International Universities Press, pp. 240-243.

Waldhorn, H. F. (1960), Assessment of analyzability: technical and theoretical observations. *Psychoanal. Quart.,* 29:478-506.

Wallerstein, R. S. (1965), The goals of psychoanalysis. *J. Amer. Psychoanal. Assn.,* 13:748-770.

——— & Sampson, H. (1971), Issues in research in the psychoanalytic process. *Internat. J. Psycho-Anal.,* 52:11-50.

Weiss, J. (1967), The integration of defenses. *Internat. J. Psycho-Anal.,* 48:520-524.

Zetzel, E. R. (1956), Current concepts of transference. *Internat. J. Psycho-Anal.,* 37:369-376.

——— (1966), The analytic situation. In: *Psychoanalysis in the Americas,* ed. R. E. Littman. New York: International Universities Press, pp. 86-106.

INDEX